Can I Have the
Keys to the Car?

How Teens and Parents
Can Talk about Things
That Really Matter

Can I Have the Keys to the Car?

Terry Paulson, Ph.D.
Sean D. Paulson

Augsburg
MINNEAPOLIS

CAN I HAVE THE KEYS TO THE CAR?
How Teens and Parents Can Talk about Things That Really Matter

Copyright © 1999 Terry Paulson and Sean Paulson. All rights reserved. Except for brief quotations in critical arti-cles or reviews, no part of this book may be reproduced in any manner without prior written permission from the publisher. Write to: Permissions, Augsburg Fortress, Box 1209, Minneapolis, MN 55440.

Acknowledgments

Scripture passages marked NRSV are from the New Revised Standard Version © 1989 by the Division of Christian Education of the National Council of the Churches of Christ in the United States of America. Used by permission.

Scripture passages marked NIV are from the Holy Bible, New International Version, copyright © 1973, 1978, 1984 by International Bible Society. Used by permission of Zondervan Publishing House. All rights reserved.

Scripture passages marked CEV are from the Contemporary English Version, copyright © 1991 American Bible Society. Used by permission.

Cover photo copyright © 1999 PhotoDisc, Inc.
Cover design by David Meyer.
Book design by Michelle L. Norstad.

Library of Congress Cataloging-in-Publication Data

Paulson, Terry L.
  Can I have the keys to the car? : how teens and parents can talk
about things that really matter / Terry Paulson and Sean D. Paulson.
     p. cm.
  Includes bibliographical references.
  ISBN 0-8066-3836-2 (alk. paper)
  1. Parent and teenager—United States. 2. Fathers and sons—
United States. 3. Parenting—Religious aspects—Christianity.
I. Paulson, Sean D., 1971- . II. Title.
HQ799.15.P35 1999
306.874—dc21
                                98-53703
                                CIP

The paper used in this publication meets the minimum requirements of American National Standard for Information Sciences—Permanence of Paper for Printed Library Materials, ANSI Z329.48-1984. ♻ ™

Manufactured in the U.S.A.   AF 9-3836

03   02   01   2   3   4   5   6   7   8   9   10

*We dedicate this book to our loving family
and to God, who makes all things possible.
May the power of family, fun, and faith
be reflected in these pages.*

Contents

How to Use This Book

This is a book to help families talk about the things that really matter in life. It's about sharing the wisdom of the ages and taking the time to talk about it.

Even committed Christian families can be challenged by the frustrations, temptations, and difficulties of surviving the teen years. No one has ever said growing up is easy for any generation, and it isn't getting any easier. The combination of a fast-paced world and more available temptations forces teens to grow up more quickly than in the past. We hope that using this book will help parents and teens navigate those challenges better.

Many families wait for a crisis before they ever sit down to talk. After surveying hundreds of teens and parents, we have teamed up to write a book that will help you start a dialogue on the timeless life lessons that are most important to learn. This book covers issues ranging from sex and drugs to honesty, faith, and the value of hard work. We hope you will be inspired by the quotes and stimulated by the content, relevant Bible passages, and thoughtful questions. This book will prove that discussing things that matter doesn't have to be boring. We trust that you'll listen, learn, and laugh together.

Even if you don't agree with all we've written, it will help you think and talk about your values. The conversations you have with each other will be more important than anything we could write.

Each chapter gives you an opportunity to talk about a question that really matters to both teens and adults. The discussion can take place in a family, youth group, school, camp, or in any other setting in which teens and adults come together.

You can take the chapters in the order in which they appear or skim the Table of Contents and choose the chapters that you most want to talk about.

You might begin a chapter by reading the "family lecture" silently or aloud. Here, as father and son, we have tried to share the insights we've learned in our own family and by talking with other teens and adults. Each family member might identify the ideas he or she found most helpful. Let each person choose the quotation they liked best. Use the "Talk It Over" questions to help you work out your own answers to the life question posed in the chapter.

While all the answers you need are not in this book, many are. Some answers will come in the dialogue you have as a family. The rest you will have to discover for yourself. We're sure, with God's help, you will. We thank you in advance for taking the time to read and use our book. May you enjoy and benefit from reading it.

—Terry and Sean Paulson

Where Does God Fit into My Life?

Whether you have gone to church for years or only on Christmas, God wants to have a personal relationship with you. God is always at your side, but it is up to you to invite God to be your partner in your walk through life. All the advice we can give means very little without Christ at your side. Know him as your Savior. You can depend upon him and pray to him for support and strength. Your relationship with God can be the most important relationship you have.

You may find that the teen years will be a tough time in which to believe and have faith in Christ. Questioning goes with growing up. You will question your parents, your teachers, and your God. Your friends will even help you do that. There's nothing wrong with questioning; struggling with your faith can make it stronger.

Now, if you want proof you can see and touch, look around you and inside you. Through faith, many see God in the handiwork and beauty of all

> **"Whenever I go past a church, I always stop and visit. I want to make sure that when they carry me in, the Lord won't ask, 'Who is it?'"**
>
> ANONYMOUS

his creations. But to make it personal, put your hands together. You're touching the hands the Lord has made. You are the proof. You are a unique gift of God, not a random product of chance. God also will continue to reveal himself to you. He has given us the Bible, the Word of God then and now. You can read it yourself. Let God speak to you as he has to believers for centuries.

God also reveals himself through other believers in the family of God. Who are the Christians you most respect? How does their faith make a difference in their lives? How has their faith made an impact on you? The biggest compliment you could pay them is to learn from them as your faith grows.

Some would say that believing in God takes all the fun out of life. Don't believe it! God's not here to punish you or zap you from the heavens. God's here to bring you joy and peace. Peace is that feeling of restful comfort that comes in knowing that God is watching and he cares.

Many parents will ask you to worship with them; others won't go near a church. We hope you'll find a church that lets you have fun in your faith and explore what God has to say to you. Whatever church you choose, be active and have the courage to

> **"Do you not know? Have you not heard? The Lord is the everlasting God, the Creator of the ends of the earth. He will not grow tired or weary, and his understanding no one can fathom. He gives strength to the weary and increases the power of the weak. Even youths grow tired and weary, and young men stumble and fall; but those who hope in the Lord will renew their strength. They will soar on wings like eagles; they will run and not grow weary, they will walk and not be faint."**
>
> ISAIAH 40:28-31 (NIV)

ask the questions you have. God can handle your honesty even when some people can't. Use your youth group as a support during your tough times. If your church doesn't have a youth group, help start one. A strong group can help keep your faith steady.

It's easy to come to God when you are in trouble. When things aren't going well, we all want God on our side. That may be why the words "Fear not!" are repeated together more than 100 times in the Bible. God is always there to give you strength.

> **"Act as if everything depends on you. And pray as if everything depends on God."**
>
> OPRAH WINFREY'S FATHER

Keep Christ with you in your victories as well. Nothing will start your day off better than thanking God for another day. Every day is a gift.

Don't forget the power of prayer. As Martin Luther once said, "To be a Christian without prayer is no more possible than to be alive without breathing." The Scriptures challenge us to pray constantly. Talk to God as you would a friend. God doesn't need big or fancy words. Just speak from your heart. You will feel God's presence.

God cares about you personally. God cared enough to give his Son, who lived and died for us. God understands our fears and our anxieties and reaches out to each of us with love. In a world that feels like it's in the fast lane, God has staying power and the promise of meaning and salvation. Remember the words of Leslie Parrott: "God's sanctuary is anywhere you and I stop long enough to meet him."

Do you have to wear God all over your jacket?

Most parents are proud of their child's expressions of faith, but we found out in our family that it could be taken to an extreme. When Sean asked me for my old trenchcoat, I did not hesitate, but to see the coat transformed into a walking Christian billboard was quite a surprise. But then, the bold statement, "God Rules!" accompanied by crosses and Christian band names seemed a rebellion that was not worth a battle. If you have to make a scene as a teen, making a scene for God seems to be a healthy compromise.

TALK IT OVER

1. What reason do you have for believing in God?

2. Where does your faith make the most difference to you?

3. What is prayer for? When do you pray? How does it make a difference?

4. What is the role of the Bible in your life? What are your favorite verses and why?

5. What Christian do you most look up to? Why? What have you learned from him or her?

"One thing I learned was that one teeny ounce of faith is worth all the training in the world."

NAVY LT. JEFFREY ZAUN, GULF WAR POW

What Does God Want Me to Do with My Life?

Taking pride in who you are and striving to be the best God wants you to be does not mean you have to make it to the Olympics or make a lot of money to count in this world. Being the best you can be has more to do with believing in yourself and searching to find and develop your own strengths that God has given you. That is your journey, and only you can take it.

Unfortunately, there is no instruction plan anyone can give you to discover your unique gifts. You are more likely to find them as you actively pursue life and all its opportunities. No one can be the best at everything, but you can start to pinpoint your strengths. Listen to your heart and your mind. Ask yourself:

> **"Whatever your hand finds to do, do it with all your might."**
>
> ECCLESIASTES 9:10 (NIV)

- What do you enjoy doing?
- What are you good at?
- What ignites a spark in you when you talk about it?
- What do people compliment you for?

Some people will notice your strengths before you do. Trust God that some skills will naturally surface, and you will know and feel it—"Hey, I'm good at this! It's me, and I love it!" The goal is to make a difference and enjoy it. The rest will take care of itself.

One of the most important lessons of life is to make sure you are searching for and working on your own dreams. Let's face it, you have to be with yourself a lot longer than you will have to be with any other person. Parents, teachers, and friends will encourage you, but don't let their encouragement drive you to discouragement by forcing you into areas you don't enjoy. Listen to their words and appreciate their encouragement because they may see gifts you are not yet aware of. But even well meaning people can be wrong. Instead of just going along with it and hating it, tell them your own dreams and involve them in helping you get there.

"Don't listen to those who say, 'You're taking too big a chance'. . . . Most important, don't listen when the little voice of fear inside you rears its ugly head and says, 'They're all smarter than you out there'. . . . I firmly believe that if you follow a path that interests you . . . with the strength of conviction, that you can move others by your own efforts, and do not make success or failure the criteria by which you live, the chances are you'll be a person worthy of your own respect."

NEIL SIMON

Even when you find your strengths, achieving anything of real value is seldom easy. Success often takes sustained sacrifice, years of learning, and precious time. Most successful people didn't get there by birthright, by winning a lottery, or by cheating. They got there by working hard to be at the right place with the right skills. In fact, Henry Ford knew the sad truth: "Whatever you have, you must either use or lose."

Larry Bird, a great basketball player and coach, knew the work behind being the best when he said, "To me, a winner is someone who recognizes his God-given talents, works his tail off to develop them into skills, and uses those skills to accomplish his goals. Even when I lost, I learned what my weaknesses were, and I went out the next day to turn those weaknesses into strengths."

> **"To me, a winner is someone who recognizes his God-given talents, works his tail off to develop them into skills, and uses those skills to accomplish his goals. Even when I lost, I learned what my weakness were, and I went out the next day to turn those weaknesses into strengths."**
>
> LARRY BIRD

Put sweat and sacrifice into your image of success; they almost always belong there. Learn to accept setbacks and gradual progress as you develop your God-given talents. Keep your expectations and goals realistic.

Master your gifts one step at a time. It's been said that if you read one hour a day in an area of interest, you could be an expert in that field within five years. Think about where you want to be an expert. Break your dreams of being the best you can be into small steps, and then start by taking the first step.

You might ask, "How does God guide my life's plan?" Like all of God's children, you will discover God's plan by reading the Bible, taking time for prayer, and trusting God's Holy Spirit to work through you to use your gifts.

Norman Vincent Peale once said, "One of the basic laws of human existence is: find yourself, know yourself, be yourself." Welcome to that challenge of finding your special place in God's plan. The people of God have been making a difference for centuries. This is your century. This is your turn to make a difference. Find and work your gifts and you will do just that.

"For whatever reason, God has blessed me with acting ability. I just try to fulfill my part of the bargain, which is to give back and to be a positive influence on others. That's all you can do: take what you've been given and spread it around. I was the middle child of three in a motivated, hard-working family. My father was a Church of God In Christ minister and my mother owned a beauty shop. There was a lot of drama, a lot of theater in my family, but I was also proud that I had to earn my money and buy my own clothes lay-away.'"

DENZEL WASHINGTON

"Do your own work well, and then you will have something to be proud of. But don't compare yourself with others. We each must carry our own load."

GALATIANS 6:4-5 (CEV)

TALK IT OVER

1. Who are people you look up to who have worked hard to be the best they can be? What do you admire most about them?

2. Share what makes you unique. List the first five things that come to mind and discuss them.

3. When Jesus walked the earth, he did not go to the rich, the famous, or the powerful to bring about his kingdom. He went to a tax collector and to fishermen and used their skills to help change the world. As God comes to you today, what gifts do you feel you have that God can use to create God's kind of world?

How Can I Have More Self-Confidence?

There's a song that says: "I get knocked down, but I get up again!" One of the most important lessons in life is learning how to treat yourself like the child of God you are. In many cases, we are nicer to others than we are to ourselves. The former First Lady, Eleanor Roosevelt, said, "No one can make me feel inferior but myself." Sure, others can help make you feel bad by things they say or do, but you, and only you, can control how you feel at the end of the day. Instead of beating yourself up and doubting whether or not you're going to make it, struggle to find a way to believe in yourself and the gifts God has given you.

> **"An occasional compliment is necessary to keep up one's self-respect. . . . When you cannot get a compliment any other way, pay yourself one."**
>
> MARK TWAIN

How do you lose your confidence? It is good to know how you can lose it before you can work on keeping it. Look at your self-confidence as the collection of all the things you say to yourself about yourself. That's right, most of us aren't kind when we talk to ourselves. Do any of these sound familiar:

- "That was stupid! Why did I say that?"
- "Oh great! They were all watching me. I'm sure they are going home tonight and talking about me over dinner!"
- "If God is watching what I did, I'm history!"

Then you have these little gremlins in the back of your mind whose sole job is to store and retrieve all of your past failures. If you don't keep your gremlin in check, he whispers in your ear, "You're right, Boss! You are stupid! Remember the other time you . . . ?"

We all know how to be tough on ourselves, but what do we say to ourselves when things go right? "It was a fluke!" "I could have done it better." "It's about time!" "I should have done this weeks ago." Even

> **"In quietness and in trust shall be your strength."**
>
> ISAIAH 30:15 (NRSV)

when we do feel good, those feelings tend not to last too long. When you get inside the average mind, most of us are far more hurtful than we are supportive of ourselves.

You don't have to lose if you can learn how to treat yourself better. First, don't take yourself for granted. God doesn't. God loves you just as you are, and he rejoices in your growth. Join God in catching yourself doing things right every day. Whether you discuss it together with family or friends or by yourself, answer this question daily: "What did I do today that I felt proud of?" You might even write about it in your journal. If you're not catching yourself being effective, you may be winning and not know it because you're not keeping score.

Secondly, when you do make mistakes, treat yourself like someone you care about. You will still have your bad days. Just make sure that you try to make every mistake an opportunity to grow. Life is like a moving vehicle with no brakes; if you spend too much time in the rearview mirror, you will hit a tree in front of you. That's why the rearview mirror is smaller than the front window. It's hard to imagine driving a car with a huge rearview mirror and only a six-inch window for seeing the road ahead. It's the same thing with life. Start by identifying what you did wrong in the past. Be specific and focus on what you actually did. It's always easier to admit you made a mistake than to admit you are one. Then, put most of your focus on what you can do about your mistake. Ask yourself: "What can I do to fix the problem? How can I handle it better next time?"

> **"Don't let anyone make fun of you, just because you are young. Set an example for other followers by what you say and do, as well as by your love, faith, and purity."**
>
> 1 TIMOTHY 4:12 (CEV)

No matter what mistakes or sins you make, you are forgiven through Christ's death and resurrection. Your sins can be left at the foot of the cross. If God can forgive you, then you ought to be able to forgive yourself. In fact, no matter what others say or do, God knows the worst about you and loves you anyway. The world needs courageous Christians who don't fear making mistakes. Live boldly. Take comfort in that promise of forgiveness.

TALK IT OVER

1. Share two things you have done in the last month that you are proud of. Discuss what it felt like to do something well.

2. Share one mistake you have made in the last month and what you learned from that mistake. What specifically did you do? What could you do to fix the problem? And how would you handle it next time?

3. Discuss how your faith makes a difference in your confidence.

"It often happens that I wake at night and begin to think about a serious problem, and decide I must tell the Pope about it. Then I wake up completely and remember that I am the Pope."

POPE JOHN XXIII

Why Should I Try Something Different?

You may have had a conversation like this:

Son: "I don't want to do it!"

Father: "How are you going to know whether you'll like it if you don't even try it?"

Son: "I know I wouldn't like it! It's not me!"

Father: "You don't have to commit your life here. How about giving it a month?"

Son: "What a waste! I've got better things to do."

Many people fail to risk trying many of the new and exciting choices that are there for them to experience. They just stand on the sideline of life and watch the world pass by. Don't let that be you.

You've probably heard adults say, "I wished I'd tried learning to play the piano when I was your age!" "I could have been on the girl's basketball team, but it wasn't cool back then." Valuable years of enjoyment were lost because they didn't seize the opportunity when they had it.

Wayne Gretzky, a great hockey player, gives credit to an early coach who made him face an important life lesson: "You miss 100 percent of the shots you never take." Let's face it; in any arena of life, you can't score if you don't try. Why settle for watching from the sidelines when you can build a habit of trying and scoring your share of goals every day of your life?

Get into the habit of doing something different every day. Keeping your mind open and creative gives you an edge for the future. Change is the only game in town. You can be a "changer," or you can wait until you are "changed." It's estimated that the average high school graduate will have up to six careers in her lifetime. That's not jobs; that's *careers*. Wealth and opportunity are on the move, and success will come to those who are flexible enough to try learning new skills to match the future.

Don't believe the people who paint the future negatively. Instead, get excited about how much fun you can have exploring and finding the place God has for you in the future. As a Christian, you have an edge. You know that Jesus Christ is with you every step of the way. Invest any worry time you might have for your future into any activity that allows you to experience a new opportunity.

> **"I never stopped trying. And I never tried stopping."**
>
> DOLLY PARTON

Before you think that trying something new is a big waste of time, ask yourself, "What's the worst that can happen?" At least, you'll find one thing you don't like to do. The potential cost of experimenting with what life has to offer is small compared to what can be gained.

Instead of picturing total commitment when approaching anything new, think of trying a few small steps. Don't make trying something such a big deal. Giving something a shot helps you sample life, helps you find what turns your dreams on.

> **"You may be disappointed if you fail, but you are doomed if you don't try."**
>
> BEVERLY SILLS

It's hard to know what you want out of life without trying some of its opportunities. So, keep sampling what life has to offer.

Dr. Martin Luther King Jr. said, "I am a sinner like all of God's children, but I want to be a good man and I want to hear a voice saying to me one day, 'I take you in and bless you because you tried.'"

> **"Do not neglect the gift, which was given you through a prophetic message."**
>
> I TIMOTHY 4:14 (NIV)

By trying, you uncover more of what God's creation has for you: all those treasures, dreams, and gifts you haven't yet experienced. In the Jewish Talmud, it is said that everyone will have to account for the things God put here for each of us, but that we failed to experience and enjoy. Jesus never wanted you to hide your light under any bushel; you were to be a light to shine for all to see. Don't waste a single day of missed opportunities to experience any of God's blessings.

TALK IT OVER

1. What things have you tried in life that you didn't think you would enjoy but that now you enjoy very much?

2. Make a list of things you would like to try in your lifetime. Pick and talk about three of them.

3. What gets in the way of trying new things? What works in convincing yourself to do it anyway?

"The biggest person standing in your way is you. Others can stop you temporarily—you are the only one who can do it permanently."

ZIG ZIGLAR, MOTIVATIONAL SPEAKER

How Can I Make It through the Bad Days?

Anybody who says life is easy hasn't really lived. Whether you like it or not, life will present you with your share of bad days. You can see them as opportunities disguised as obstacles or as just another reason to complain. That's where a positive attitude makes such a big difference.

Entertain this wild thought: your happiness is not the responsibility of your parents or your teachers. It's yours. At best, their job is to help you find a way to navigate through the same ups and downs that everybody experiences on their way to adulthood. There's freedom in taking responsibility for your own attitude and your own happiness. Everyone grows

> **"Suicide is a permanent solution to a temporary problem."**
>
> ABIGAIL VAN BUREN

through adversity, and you deserve the right to face your own problems and overcome them yourself. Those who have learned to conquer their problems are more secure than those who have never faced them. That is why your attitude is so important.

At times, everyone feels discouraged, but you don't have to feel that way for long. Trust that God has a plan and get busy making your life better with whatever cards you're dealt. After all, that's all anyone can do. Henry Ford once said, "If you think you can, or if you think you can't, you are right." Invest any time you might waste thinking "I can't" into any action that can make things better. People with a positive attitude don't just think positively; they are doers who struggle, fight, and claw their way through whatever obstacles they encounter.

> **"Athletics teaches you that you've got to overcome adversity. Nobody goes unbeaten every year; nobody makes every shot; no one sinks every putt. Everybody's going to have problems. I've been on top; I've been on the bottom. I've learned that success is never final; defeat is not fatal. Whether it's in business, on the field, or in your personal life, the person who copes with problems and uses them as motivation is going to be successful."**
>
> LOU HOLTZ, FORMER FOOTBALL COACH, NOTRE DAME

If you do face tough times that are bigger than you think you can handle, don't pick that time to make big decisions alone. Trust that God will put the right people in your life to help you. When things seem tough, find someone you trust to help you figure it out. Talking with adults often provides insightful perspectives that years of experience can produce. You may soon find that you are not alone, even in your own home. After all, as old as they look, your parents were your age once themselves. Parents can help you bounce back from even the worst experience. If given a chance, most people would love to serve as coach and cheerleader on the sidelines of your life. Have no doubt about it: they want you to succeed. Sometimes you may not want to talk to your parents. Try a minister, a trusted friend or even a teacher you respect. Talk to someone; it will make a difference.

Never leave God out of the equation. God is always there to listen and give you strength. You can call on him and his promises of strength and guidance. You may have heard it asked, "If God be for me, who can be against me?" God's being for you doesn't mean there will always be good times. Sometimes bad things happen to good people. But God is with us through the tough times to help us become stronger. You can trust that there are no problems too big for God.

"Action is a great restorer and builder of confidence. Inaction is not only the result, but the cause of fear. Perhaps the action you take will be successful; perhaps different action or adjustments will have to follow. But any action is better than no action at all. So don't wait for trouble to intimidate or paralyze you. Make a move."

NORMAN VINCENT PEALE

The Bible is living testimony to this truth. Its pages do not come from people living in any Garden of Eden. The Psalms were born out of difficulty. Some of the Epistles were written from prison. The Bible is a book of reality. And reality can be difficult. Like believers of old, life will at times bend you, but it won't break you if you learn to trust in God, even during your darkest hours.

Do not forget the power of gratitude and thanksgiving. Unrealistic expectations are a sure road to unhappiness and disappointment.

Optimists, however, hope for more, but are not thrown by less. Underneath their healthy persistence is a sense of appreciation for the gifts of life they receive every day. Learn to count your blessings. Try saying in the face of stress, "I'm blessed out today." And never forget the words of Reinhold Niebuhr's often quoted *Serenity Prayer*: "God grant me the serenity to accept the things I cannot change, the courage to change the things I can, and the wisdom to know the difference."

"I recall asking her once how she managed to work from sunup to sundown, without ever once complaining about the unfairness of it all. She'd just look at me with a smile in her eyes, 'Son, life ain't always fair, but it's bearable. God ain't gonna put on you more than you can take. Life can be bitter, and it can be sweet, but the secret is to take the bitterness with the sweet.'"

EVANDER HOLYFIELD, BOXER

IF DEPRESSION WON'T GO AWAY

"People are now recognizing depression as an illness and not a character flaw." Dr. Robert Hirschfield, National Institute of Mental Health

Not all depression is the result of a bad attitude. Severe depression, in its most disabling forms, may be biologically based. This isn't a normal dip in mood that everyone experiences at times; true depression is more intense and longer lasting. Does the slightest annoyance set off irrational tantrums followed by days of lying in bed, crying, too depressed to shower or get dressed? Do you lose your appetite for extended periods of time or do the opposite, eating more than usual and sleeping for long hours? Do you have a severely depressed parent or an early loss of either parent? Do you have recurrent thoughts of death or suicide? If you find yourself answering yes to many of these questions, you may be left with more than the pain of depression. You will have the guilt of not being able to beat it. A severely depressed teen cannot simply "cheer up" or "snap out of it." Yet severe depression can often be treated successfully with expert assistance including medication and counseling. There is no future in suicide. Ask your parents, minister, or school counselor to help you find a local mental-health professional who has experience in working with depressed teens. Know that you are not alone.

TALK IT OVER

1. What helps you most in getting through tough times?

2. One of the most frequently quoted prayers of our time was written by Reinhold Niebuhr and is affectionately called the Serenity Prayer. What about yourself have you learned to accept that now has become a positive? Where have you used your positive attitude and courage to change?

3. What person from the Bible most impresses you for having a positive attitude? Why?

4. What adults would you feel most comfortable talking to if you needed support through a tough time in your life? What about them makes it easy for you to talk to them?

"You have accepted Christ Jesus as your Lord. Now keep on following him. Plant your roots in Christ and let him be the foundation for your life. Be strong in your faith, just as you were taught. And be grateful."

COLOSSIANS 2:6-7 (CEV)

What's So Funny?

A sense of humor is one of those tools God had the wisdom to give us. It will help you throughout your life. Many people walk around all day looking as if they are in pain. It's a mistake to assume that it is cool to be serious. Don't let that be you. Leave room for laughter every day. You know how fun it is to laugh about something with your friends. Laughter is contagious, but so is being negative. Which would you prefer to give to others? You know the answer. Most people love to be around others who make them laugh. Take your school and your work seriously, but take yourself and your problems lightly.

When things are going crazy, take a trip to the funny side of life. Laughter provides a natural "high," an emotional massage, a recess you can call for yourself any time, any place. Who needs drugs when you have life to laugh at.

"The cheerful heart has a continual feast."

PROVERBS 15:15 (NIV)

Learn to say to yourself and others, "Are we having fun yet?" "Don't worry! Be happy!" "Some days you're the bug; some days you're the windshield!" There is nothing wrong with crying, but why cry when you can laugh? We all need humor, parents and teens alike.

Not all humor works. Some humor creates laughter at the expense of others. Don't make fun of others. God calls us to laugh with others, not at them. Cliff Thomas once said, "When someone blushes with embarrassment, . . . when someone carries away an ache, . . . when something sacred is made to appear common, . . . when someone's weakness provides the laughter, . . . when profanity is required to make it funny, . . . when a child is brought to tears, . . . or when everyone can't join in the laughter, . . . it's a poor joke!"

> **"What really works in life is being able to bounce back. Resilience—that's what does it. If you stop and think, nothing is as bad as it seems. In the worst moments, I've always found that something funny was happening. And for that I give my mother credit. Judy Garland could cry, but she was also one of the world's great laughers."**
>
> LIZA MINELLI

The safest target for your humor will always be yourself. Learn to laugh at your errors and the world will laugh with you—not at you. A laugh at your own expense costs you nothing. After all, only the self-confident can admit their mistakes. Laughing at your own errors will help you let go of mistakes and bounce back. We all like to be with people who are comfortable with who they are—zits and all.

Humor helps make relationships work. Victor Borge once said, "Laughter is the shortest distance between two people." Relationships are like savings accounts. If you don't make deposits to the account, there is nothing to withdraw when you need it.

Using your sense of humor with others puts a deposit in your relationship account. Do it every chance you get.

A sense of humor is too important to leave to chance. Work at making humor a bigger part of your life. One thing you can do is keep a videotape of your favorite comedies and watch them when you need a lift. Use your family refrigerator or the door of your room to put up your favorite cartoons. Keep the best cartoons and funny family pictures in a photo album to share with family and friends. Keep looking for humor. Be ready to say, "That's funny! This is going to be a great story." Be the one in your family that asks, "What funny thing happened today?" Then share your own story, "A funny thing happened when . . ."

> **"The best way to cheer yourself is to try to cheer somebody else up."**
>
> MARK TWAIN

Don't worry about upsetting God with a good laugh. Laughter is a sacred sound to God. Martin Luther knew the value of a sense of humor when he said, "God is not a God of sadness, but the devil is. Christ is a God of joy. It is pleasing to God whenever you rejoice or laugh from the bottom of your heart." God calls us to claim one of the greatest gifts of the Spirit—joy.

> **"He deserves Paradise who makes his companions laugh."**
>
> THE KORAN

Nothing brings joy to the surface like a good laugh. Let there be laughter, and let it start with you.

TALK IT OVER

1. What is one of the funniest memories you
   have about growing up in your home? in your
   school? in your church?

2. Why is it important to have a sense of humor?

3. When is humor hurtful?

4. When has your sense of humor helped you
   through a tough situation?

"Everybody has used the expression, 'Someday we'll laugh about this.' My question is, why wait?"

JOEL GOODMAN

How Can I Talk So My Parents Will Listen?

P arents and teens have always had their share of disagreements, and they will continue to have them. Conflict comes with being in a family. In fact, the first commandment that promises a result is the one that reads: "Honor your father and mother, so that you may live long in the land the Lord your God is giving you." Living long sounds good. In Ephesians, Paul again tells children to obey their parents, but he also tells fathers to not overcorrect their children or make it difficult for them to obey. In God's eyes, it's important for both parents and teens to be careful about how they talk to one another.

Your parents do not plot at night to make your life miserable, but, like most parents, they do their best to provide the direction and the limits to keep you safe. Many of those limits run up against your desire for more freedom and independence. As a result, your family will sometimes feel like you're all heading into World War III. The trick is to find a way to disagree and push for what you want without starting the war.

This does not mean you have to agree with everything your parents say; that just isn't possible. It's not about letting things go unsaid either. On the other hand, it's important for you to express even some of your strongest feelings to your parents. This is a life lesson on how to be courteous, respectful, and considerate when speaking to an adult.

When you are making your point, two of the most important things to remember are your timing and the way you present it. Even when you try, it won't always be easy for either you or your parents to hear what the other has to say. But it's important to keep talking, even when it doesn't seem to be working. Perhaps you have heard a conversation like this:

Son: "Dad, you have to let me do this!"
Dad: "I don't have to do anything!"
Son: "I can't believe you won't let me go! I'm speechless."
Dad: "Is there any way you could try that just for an hour?"

Everybody gets angry at their parents. Parents have their moments too. But, no one ever promised there wouldn't be a few rocky moments. Just don't let any of those rocky moments turn into a landslide. Anger does not excuse hateful comments by you or your parents. It's been said that anger is a wind which blows out the lamp of the mind.

> **"Everyone should be quick to listen, slow to speak, and slow to become angry."**
>
> JAMES 1:19 (NIV)

When you feel you're going to say something you'll regret, follow the old suggestion and count to ten before you speak. Take time to get out of the situation; go to your room *before* you're sent there. Taking time alone doesn't show weakness; it shows wisdom. Let your parents know what you're doing *before you leave.* Say, "Look, I don't want to say anything I'll regret. Can I go to my room for a few minutes to calm down and think? I'll talk to you, but let me think it through for a few minutes." Once in your room, take a few deep breaths, and then think about what you want to say. If you are still struggling with strong feelings, try writing some of your thoughts and feelings on paper or call a friend to talk about how to handle the problem. Writing and talking will help you control your emotions and help you give a better message when you do talk to your parents.

"When you lose your temper—you really lose something. You lose the ability to think sanely and to make balanced decisions."

GEORGE SWEETING

Whatever you say, the most important thing is to make sure you come back to talk the problem through. Most parents will try to give you the distance and time you need, but they won't want to avoid important conversations. Keep in mind when you're taking time that parents also may need some time to cool down. You'll have better luck getting through to your parents when they're calm than when they're in a shouting match with you.

When you do go back to talk, there are a few things to remember. Try avoiding statements like "everyone else," "It's all your fault," "It's not fair!" Avoid bringing up other parents. You have your parents as parents. Use your head in choosing words that will work for them and build a case for your position. Don't talk about blame; talk about what both you and your parents can do now and in the future to take care of problems. Because you have a mind of your own, you can use it to help find a solution that works.

Carefully choose which things you want to disagree about. There will be many times that you and your parents will see things very differently, but people can learn to *agree to disagree*. It takes two to argue. If one side steps out of the argument, there is no reason to continue. Instead of overreacting to your parent's advice, learn that there are some battles you aren't going to win. You can always think to yourself that you are right and still let your parents express their point of view. Try a simple statement, such as, "I don't know if we will ever agree on this, but I know you're only saying what you think is best for me. I'll have to think some more about it."

It's not always your fault when things go badly. If your parents fail to listen or are just plain wrong, don't try to force them to admit it in the heat of battle. Such tactics seldom work. Former President Calvin Coolidge said wisely, "I have never been hurt by anything I didn't say." Give your parents the time and the space they need to calm down.

> **"A gentle answer turns away wrath, but a harsh word stirs up anger."**
>
> PROVERBS 15:1 (NIV)

Most of the time, your parents will tell you that you have gone far enough. When parents harshly say no, this is not the time to push. You know how it feels to have a friend keep asking you for something you've already told him or her you won't give. Your parents feel the same way when you push too hard. As we have already said, you are more likely to get your way by building a good case for your position and giving them time to think.

Learn to disagree without being disagreeable. Learn to make your case without hammering it home. In time, all your decisions will be your own. Working at communicating now will help you in future relationships. Remember, even important arguments are seldom worth hurting someone you love. Don Herold understood this when he said, "Don't ever slam a door; you might want to go back."

"Do not let any unwholesome talk come out of your mouths, but only what is helpful for building others up according to their needs, that it may benefit those who listen."

EPHESIANS 4:29 (NIV)

TALK IT OVER

1. Talk about a time your parents changed their minds because of the way you made your point. What did you do that worked?

2. "Fighting words" are words people use that are guaranteed to make the other person angry. What are some of the fighting words that make you most angry?

3. Talk about a time you were glad your parents didn't give in.

4. How could these principles for good communication be applied to situations at school, at work, or in other organizations?

How Can I Find Real Friends?

Friends are important; they help make life enjoyable. With friends you'll learn how to listen, how to share ideas, and how to share feelings with someone who cares. A friend is there to laugh and have fun with, even to handle hurts and disappointments. Some of the friends you have now will be yours for life. Enjoy making memories together. You don't need lots of good friends, but life goes more smoothly with at least a few.

Be yourself! Good friends will respect that. Bill Cosby once said, "I don't know the key to success, but the key to failure is trying to please everybody." Don't try and win people over by being someone you're not. By sharing your true interests, your own opinions and your most important dreams, you will find those friends who like you as you are. Such friends often last a lifetime.

> **"It is better to be alone than in bad company."**
>
> GEORGE WASHINGTON

If you tend to be shy, you're not alone. But when you act shy, you miss out on meeting many friends you could have had, and they miss out in getting to know how much you have to offer. Try a sure way to gradually break out of your shyness: smile as you walk through life.

Go beyond the smile to say "Hi" to someone new. Pretend you're responsible for not letting others feel shy. The best way to do that is to show interest in them and to be a good, enthusiastic listener. Soon you'll find plenty of new friends worth keeping, and you'll have fun doing it.

There is truth in the statement, "You're known by the company you keep." It's natural to pick up habits from friends you spend time with. Some of those habits will work for you; some habits can get you in trouble. Most parents will let you know when the actions of your friends concern them, but don't wait for your parents to try to control you or your friends. Learn to do that yourself.

Bring your friends to your home. Let your parents get to know them, so they can appreciate the strengths you find in them. When they get to know your friends, it is easier for them to move beyond their doubts to trust your judgment. To help build trust more quickly, understand that most parents expect you to be responsible for your friends' conduct when in your house. Take time to let your friends know what is expected

> **"Keep away from negative people who try to belittle your ambitions. Small people always do that, but the really great make you feel that you, too, can become great."**
>
> MARK TWAIN

from them in your house before it becomes a problem.

While we are talking about friends, don't use "peer pressure" as an excuse for any choices you make. In the first place, no matter what the age or group, the pressure to be approved by others will always be a factor. That doesn't change the fact that few parents, coaches, teachers, bosses, or judges will let you pass off your responsibility by blaming others. Your choices are *your* responsibility.

"Do not use a hatchet to remove a fly from your friend's forehead."

CHINESE PROVERB

Standing for what is right may not be as lonely a job as you think it would be. Christ is always at your side; you are never alone in taking a stand. Most friends you will spend time with also want to do what is right. They will act that way when they have a positive example to follow. If you have the courage to stand for your convictions even when pushed, you will give others the encouragement they need to stand along with you.

Just like God, you can be a good friend through the good times *and* the bad. Don't expect that any friendship will always be clear sailing. No relationship ever is. Be able to confront a good friend privately when they don't see their own mistakes. With time, they will see what a true friend you are. Ask them to do the same with you. A good

"Whoever walks with the wise becomes wise, but the companion of fools suffers harm."

PROVERBS 13:20 (NRSV)

friend cares enough to let you know you're making a mistake *before* you make a fool of yourself. Lousy friends tell you the good news to your face and the bad news to others behind your back. Don't be that kind of friend. Don't put up with friends who do that to you.

To have a good friend, be one. Instead of envying the gifts your friends have, celebrate their achievements. Instead of competing with them, be excited for them. Instead of being concerned about your needs alone, take time to care about theirs. In short, bring out the best in your friends by leaving them better for having known you. We might do well to start every day with the same prayer Ben Franklin used: "Thank you Lord for the success of my friends and the fewness of my enemies! May all my friends achieve their fondest dreams."

"As a young girl growing up in the South, I would hear my grandmother singing an old Girl Scout song: 'Make new friends but keep the old—one is silver, and the other is gold.' The older I get, the more I realize how this simple rhyme expresses one of the best lessons I've ever learned. Friends make the bad times easier and the good times sweeter. Friends—the kind that are with you 'through thick and thin'—can remind you of who you are. Success and good times don't matter much unless you have friends with whom you can share them."

ALEXIS HERMAN, U.S. SECRETARY OF LABOR

1. Name one person you consider a good friend. Why did you choose that person to be your friend?

2. What qualities make a person a good friend?

3. What's the best way you've found to meet good friends?

4. What does it mean to stand up for a friend? How would you handle it if they did something wrong?

5. If one of your friends described the reason they valued your friendship, what would they say?

Where did you get that game?

New games don't just appear out of nowhere, and guilt has a way of surfacing the truth. So when Sean came to us to report receiving merchandise that his friend had stolen, the lesson learned said as much about picking good friends as it did about honesty. Having to take back the item cemented the memory forever and ended a friendship that wasn't worth keeping.

Who Needs Good Manners?

Why do I have to worry about how I hold my fork? Who cares anyway?" Your parents probably said the same thing to their parents, and there is a reason that manners are important. Lillian Gish said it best: "You can get through life with bad manners, but it's easier with good manners." Knowing the rules of the "social game" gives you an advantage in a world that cares about first impressions.

Why learn good manners? It's simple. You may already be experiencing the sometimes painful passage of moving from teenager to adult. Bosses will expect you to know how to act, so you don't scare away customers. "What's happenin', man?" somehow doesn't stack up with, "Good morning. Can I help you, sir?" You will soon grow into a young man or woman who is less concerned about the current trends and more concerned about finding a good job and a husband or wife who can help you be successful and happy. Now, if getting a job

> **"Let us therefore make every effort to do what leads to peace and to mutual edification."**
>
> ROMANS 14:19 (NIV)

that you love doing doesn't inspire you, think about those dates you may be missing because you turned off that person or, even worse, his or her parents.

There seem to be few universal manners you can trust. What is right in one group may be a sign of rudeness

> **"Manners are a sensitive awareness of the feelings of others. If you have that awareness, you have good manners, no matter what fork you use."**
>
> EMILY POST

and lack of respect in another. Making a good impression in another country is tough. You learn when to bow, when to speak, whether to shake hands, and whether a burp is a sign of respect or just being crude.

That brings us to the heart of having good manners. There is no one correct way. Be more concerned about doing what is appropriate to the group you are with. Emily Post, an author of many books on etiquette, made that clear when she said, "Manners are a sensitive awareness of the feelings of others. If you have that awareness, you have good manners, no matter what fork you use." Just caring enough to fit into a group's manners is a sign of respect.

> **"Manners will take you places money can't. . . . It's not a replacement for character; it's a reflection of it. It's an art."**
>
> MARJABELLE YOUNG STEWART, THE "QUEEN OF COURTESY"

Instead of waiting to be told how to act, you can observe and learn from others who have social graces. In unfamiliar groups, play it safe. Don't be the first to act; let others show you the way. If you're a guest at a home, you can always look to the hostess for guidelines on how to act.

Being courteous and polite is not limited to how loud you play your music. It has to do with an attitude of concern for the feelings and sensitivities of others. This list may seem silly, but is not any less important: put the toilet seat down and flush before leaving: clean up the crumbs after you snack; put your dirty clothes in the hamper; be gentle instead of blunt; open doors for others; and, of course, take time to say, "thank you," "please," and "I'm sorry." When you show courtesy, it will usually bring courtesy in return.

A good first impression on the job doesn't stop with good manners, how you dress and look makes a difference as well. Dressing in the latest fad, wearing nine earrings on each ear, or trying the newest hair style may work with your friends, but it may not get you where you want to go in the

> **"Introducing yourself to others, shaking their hands, and making eye contact are all part of being polite and letting others know that you are interested."**
>
> DR. PHILIP G. ZIMBARDO AND SHIRLEY RADL

adult world. On most jobs you're likely to hear: "You can't work here looking like that. If you want to get a job, you'd better learn to dress the part." They won't hire you, and why should they? Too much is at stake on the first impressions employees make with customers. As Will Rogers liked to say, "You don't get a second chance at a first impression."

Your One-Stop Guide to Table Manners

"'Which is my water glass?' 'Is that your salad plate?' 'What is that crazy knife [for] anyway?' Unfortunately by the time such queries are raised, the people raising them are already seated at formally set tables and on the verge of embarrassing themselves beyond repair. If you follow the simple rules listed below, you'll never again have to pretend you're not hungry.

Rule 1: RSVP, ASAP. RSVP as soon as possible. When you have responded by phone or mail, . . . you have entered into a `sacred contract.'

Rule 2: Roll with the punches. Roll on the left. Water on the right. Now sear that information into your gray matter.

Rule 3: Work your way in. Begin eating with the outside utensil then work your way in.

Rule 4: Don't fuss about food. Food fussing . . . is one of this decades' major dinner faux pas [errors]."

Miss Manners, Judith Martin

1. Share some examples of good manners that are appropriate in one society but not in another.

2. Who do you look up to as a model for making a good impression? Why?

3. If you wanted to get a job or make a good impression, how would you change your appearance? How would you act differently?

What about that mohawk haircut?

Sean just didn't understand why a self-styled Mohawk haircut wasn't the look of choice for the Paulson household. But he soon found that a good old-fashioned buzz cut supplied by a less than happy father would provide a suitable alternative.

You Want Me Home by When?

What could all of you do in your home to be more courteous? Almost all teens have heard the words: "As long as you are under this roof, you will. . . ." Then out comes a local version of the house rules. With that in mind, you may be surprised by how many parents look forward to giving you more and more freedom on your way to adulthood. You want that as well. You're tired of being a teenager, and that's healthy. You will have all the freedom you want in a few years. You also will have the responsibility and choices that go with that freedom. Will you keep going to school? What will you do to pay the bills? Who you will marry? No parent, even though they may try, can make those choices for you. But you're not at that point yet. While you are still living at home, if you want more freedom, you may have to earn it.

What's in it for you? You will earn more freedom. When you let your parents know where you are and when you arrive home in time for curfew, you earn your parents' trust. When you have your parents' trust, more freedom usually follows.

When you were a child, your parents were used to protecting you, watching your every move, and making sure you didn't get hurt. They were sure that if they turned their backs, even for one minute, you may become lost. Even though you are older, don't expect your parents' fears to go away easily. Work with them, and it will be easier for them to gradually let go. When you fight them, they tend to hold on tighter. Humor them by giving them the information that they need to know you're safe. Your parents care. Be glad they do.

Parents need information to trust your judgment. Give them the information they need before they even ask for it. Keep them informed wherever you go with a simple note, a quick phone call, or a message on their answering machine or beeper. It doesn't take much. Most parents understand that sometimes they're not that easy to check in with. They live busy lives as well, and that makes it even more important to tell them your plans early. Over time, as they develop more trust, you will be able to do less checking in and more reporting on where you have been.

> **"Our privileges can be no greater than our obligations. The protection of our rights can endure no longer than the performance of our responsibilities."**
>
> JOHN F. KENNEDY

Respecting your curfew is no different. Most parents understand that even with the best of planning on your part, you will occasionally be late. But don't push the limits by making it a habit. If it becomes a frequent problem, it just might get harder to get out of your room. Curfews aren't punishments; they give parents and teens a way to test judgment and dependability. As parents gain trust, you gain confidence in your own ability to honor your commitments.

Trust is like a bank account. When you act responsibly, you keep adding deposits. When you are distrustful, you make withdrawals. The quicker you act the less trust you lose. So, don't wait until the last minute to tell your parents you'll be late. Asking for more time early is always your best bet.

If you are late, be ready to take your medicine. Surprise your parents. Take responsibility by facing the consequences and promising to do better next time. Then do it. Just as your heavenly Father promises to forgive your sins when you repent, so, too, will your parents when you sincerely admit your mistakes. Forgiveness does not mean that you won't have to face the consequences for your actions; it just means that you get a new start from which to build.

"My mother usually waited up for me after a high school date. If she was too tired, however, she would leave a 'welcome home' note, which always read: 'Wake me up when you come in because you know I can't sleep a wink until you're home.'"

PATTI B. HIATT

When you honor your curfew and let your parents know where you are, you can borrow on your trust bank account. Start today to keep your "trust account" in good standing.

TALK IT OVER

1. Let the adults answer this one: What were the rules in your home when you were teenagers? Which were the hardest for you to follow?

2. What are the curfew rules in your house?

3. Why does it make sense for both parents and children to let others know where they are?

4. If you are going to be late, what should you do?

5. What can you do to increase your "trust account"?

"If you don't confess your sins, you will be a failure. But God will be merciful if you confess your sins and give them up."

PROVERBS 28:13 (CEV)

Did You Say "SEX"?

Sex is not dirty, and it's not evil. Sexual intercourse is a powerful, sensual, and spiritual experience that is wonderful at the right time and with the right person. We would also be lying if we said that experimenting with sex can't be exciting. Having sex before marriage may not ruin your life, but having intercourse outside of marriage is a sin and should never be taken lightly.

Many young people in America have had sex, and, admittedly, most have survived. They often act on the belief that if two people love each other and are serious about the relationship, there is nothing wrong with having sex. Unfortunately, in practice, that usually means people will have a series of sexual partners, because many close relationships will break up. As much as you are sure of your love for someone, you will probably go through many close relationships held together only by your current feelings.

That leaves us with an important question. Is having sex with all the people you are "serious about" the best way to experience sex? God's plan is for you to save sex for marriage. The more people you have sex with before marriage, the harder it is to make intimacy in marriage special. If marriage means less, it offers less. When you give sex freely, what do you give when it is special?

Words like commitment and abstinence aren't often appreciated in our society; they aren't even seen as practical. You'll see sex with a condom promoted a great deal. As a result of the promotion of safer sex, your choice to have sex is even more likely to be tested.

> **"When the time comes for me to leave home, I want my parents to say, 'I wonder what my daughter will become,' not 'What will become of my daughter?'"**
>
> YASMIN RICE

When you say no, be ready with what else you will say. Try any of these: "No, I've promised God that I will wait until I am married." "No, that's not what I want." "No, I am waiting until I'm married." In fact, saying no repeatedly with increasing volume has a pretty strong impact.

It may help you to know that millions of others your age feel the same way you do and have decided not to have sex before marriage. Campaigns, such as, "True Love Waits," have been making a difference by providing pledge cards and support for teens who want to take a stand for abstinence.

> **"Nobody's ever died from not having sex. It's the one appetite that's not necessary to fulfill."**
>
> KATHLEEN SULLIVAN

When someone says you are "not normal," you can reply with conviction, "I never asked to be average." If someone says, "You would if you really loved me," you can be sure that's only a line. If your date says, "Everybody does it," be ready to say, "Then you won't have trouble finding someone else to do it with." Having sex will not cure loneliness, and it will not make you popular for the right reasons. Saying no can give you the gift of freedom.

> **"Flee from sexual immorality. All other sins a man commits outside his body, but he who sins sexually sins against his own body. Do you not know that your body is a temple of the Holy Spirit, who is in you, whom you have received from God? You are not your own; you were bought at a price. Therefore, honor God with your body."**
>
> I CORINTHIANS 6:18-20 (NIV)

Young men, don't buy or perpetuate myths of desire— "Women want to be pushed," or, more commonly, "'No' really means `Yes'!" Forced sex is rape! The choice to have sex is something no one should force. Pushing sex on an unwilling partner is not a game; it's a crime.

Young women, don't count on the fact that your date has read this book. Take responsibility for your own actions. Avoid drinking or dressing provocatively on dates. If you put yourself in a situation where it's easier for your date to lose control, it is still rape, but it doesn't make sense to increase the odds. Until you know a person well, plan for safe dates. Arrange to have a friend at a party that you can ride home with. If you have a good friend you trust, double date to have someone to help keep things in control. It's never wise to wait for passion to make the choice for either of you.

Can you be close without having intercourse? Yes! Physical closeness does not require having intercourse. Holding, cuddling, caressing, and kissing are other ways of being close without having sex. Saying no to intercourse is not saying no to all contact. If you've made the choice to not have sex before you're married and still be physically close, you had better be ready to pull out the old stop sign or know how to apply your own brakes. It won't hurt you to use those brakes. As Kathleen Sullivan once said, "Nobody's ever died from not having sex. It's the one appetite that's not necessary to fulfill."

The best contraceptive remains saying no. But even good advice isn't always heard. That leaves many parents with an uncomfortable message to tell their children: "Save sex for marriage, but if you're going to have sex, take precaution to make it as safe as possible."

The sad fact is that most sexually active teenagers don't use birth control or contraceptives the first time they have intercourse. Unfortunately, all it takes is one time that you don't use birth control for a pregnancy to result. It only takes one time to get a sexually transmitted disease. Is this meant to scare you? Yes, it is! You can't look into the eyes of someone and tell if they have a disease. Unfortunately, many sexually transmitted diseases can cause a lifetime of problems, and some, if not treated, can cause death.

Talking openly about sex still requires knowing something about birth control options. Just as having a seat belt does not mean anyone condones driving recklessly, knowing about birth control protection does not mean you have to have sex before marriage.

No matter what you read, taking precautions is not "safe sex." At best, it is "safer sex." Reducing the risk will never be the same as eliminating the risk. Except for abstinence, fail-safe protection does not exist. The choice remains yours.

No matter what you decide, it's hard to go through these temptations alone. You may be able to talk with your parents. But, if you find it hard to talk to them, find an adult you trust and respect from church or school. An adult relative might also be willing to listen. Talk to someone. Knowing they understand can help you make the tough choices.

"When you go to bed with one man, you go to bed with his entire sexual history, and the history of all his sexual partners."

ELLEN GOODMAN

If you have already had sex, it is not too late to become a "spiritual virgin" again. Through prayer, God promises to forgive us and cleanse us for a fresh start. To the woman caught in adultery, Jesus gave a freeing message of new life: ". . . neither do I condemn you. Go and sin no more." Your vow of abstinence can start today. Claim God's plan to wait for that special person you will marry.

TALK IT OVER

1. Why is it hard to talk with parents about sex? What would make it easier?

2. What are the reasons that make the most sense to you for saving sex for marriage?

3. What have you learned about saying no? How would you put on the brakes?

"I want to enjoy being a child, not raising one."

KATIE PANTOJA

If Everybody Else Lies, Why Should I Tell the Truth?

T hink of your best friends. Do you trust them? Sure you do, or they wouldn't be good friends. You don't need a long lecture on telling the truth, because you know how it feels to have someone not keep their word. You probably don't like it when your friends lie to you. Does that help you understand why it is so important that you tell the truth?

It's not easy to stand for telling the truth. There are too many excuses that make it easy for people to take the easy way out. Have you heard any of these statements to defend lying? "Everything is relative!" "Everyone does it!" "If I tell the truth, I will hurt their feelings!" "What they don't know won't hurt them." The attitude that seems very prevalent today with some teens and adults, is that it's OK to lie, *if you can get away with it.*

Some teens say, "Parents aren't friends—they're parents. You're supposed to lie to parents." But parents are people too. You and your parents are in this together for the long haul whether you like

"If you tell the truth, you don't have to remember anything."

MARK TWAIN

it or not. Many of your friends in high school will move out of your life; your parents will hopefully be with you for a lifetime.

The short-lived relief we get from lying will never make up for the trust we lose. It takes a history to build trust; it can take only one lie to destroy that history. If you sneak around, you make parents become detectives. Besides, you don't want your parents lying to you. That's no way for any family to live.

Honesty may be painful at times, but it's always the best way to go. Mark Twain identified an added advantage to honesty, "If you tell the truth, you don't have to remember anything."

> **"No man has a good enough memory to make a successful liar."**
>
> ABRAHAM LINCOLN

What about "white lies"? Before you convince yourself to lie, make sure that if others ever found out most would understand why you lied. If you would be embarrassed for others to find out, it is not a "white lie." Pursue truth whenever and wherever important commitments are involved. Stand your ground, even when no one else seems to be with you. God is with you. God wants you to be known for the promises you keep, not for the ones you have broken.

You might be saying to yourself, "But I've already told so many lies. Why read on?" You're not alone; most of us have had to learn the hard way that truth is the best course to take. It's never too late to build an honest future starting today. It starts with the gift of forgiveness and moves to a new commitment to change. God forgives and challenges us to "go and sin no more."

There is a treasure to be found in being honest. Plato said, "Truth is its own reward." No matter what your past or what you end up doing with your life, your character can be an asset that all will respect. Treat it as a treasure. Be known as a "promise keeper," and that trait alone will assure your success in any career or relationship. People want to work and live with people they can count on.

As for your parents, they want to trust you, and you want to trust them. Most parents will do their best to be honest with you and maintain your trust. We have all seen too many parents and teens who don't trust each other. Once they lose that trust, it takes a long time to gain it back. Do your part, so that doesn't happen in your home.

"We are part of the same body. Stop lying and start telling each other the truth."

EPHESIANS 4:25 (CEV)

Remember, saying something that you know isn't true or covering up the truth are both lying. When you make the right choice to stand for truth, you will learn what the great UCLA basketball coach, John Wooden, tried to get through to his players, "No pillow is as soft as a clear conscience."

TALK IT OVER

1. Under what conditions are you tempted to lie?

2. How does it make you feel to be lied to? How do you feel after you've lied?

3. Why is it important to be honest and tell the truth?

4. How does your faith in God make a difference in being honest?

"I hope I shall always possess firmness and virtue enough to maintain what I consider to be the most enviable of all titles: the character of an honest man."

GEORGE WASHINGTON

How Can I Get Along with People?

T here is probably no more important lesson in life than the one expressed in Matthew 7:12, more often known as the golden rule: "So in everything, do to others what you would have them do to you, for this sums up the Law and the Prophets."

The reason it is such an important lesson is because relationships are like savings accounts. If you don't put any money in your savings account, when you want to buy something important, there is nothing there to spend. The same is true with your "people account." If you don't treat others with respect and caring, you should not be surprised when they show no concern in return. Even then, not everyone will treat you nicely. But we are called to treat others as we want to be treated, whether or not they return the favor.

Winston Churchill said, "We make a living by what we get, but we make a life by what we give." You can make a difference. Living by the golden rule means going out of your way to help people in ways you would want to be helped. It means trying to understand why people do things instead of just reacting to what they do. It means putting yourself in their position, not just demanding that they understand yours. It means asking the question, "How would I feel if someone did that to me?" This change in how you treat others may not seem like a big deal, but as Mother Teresa once said, "We can do no great things; only small things with great love."

Unfortunately, one of the easiest things to learn in this world is to hate. It's never difficult to make an enemy. Simply meeting a person on one of their worst days can create a dislike for that person. First impressions are hard to change.

Having a bad early experience is not the only way we make enemies. Sometimes we are turned off by what we fear or don't know. Everybody has grown up with some biases, but you can learn to look and live beyond them. Don't let age, gender, religion, race, wealth, job status, or nationality confuse the facts. All people are God's people. With prejudices, we expect our fears to be true. We keep our distance and then look for evidence to support our worst fears. That's why prejudice is hard to change.

> **"Kindness can become its own motive. We are made kind by being kind."**
>
> ERIC HOFFER

Whether you've had a bad experience or you've got your share of prejudiced opinions, give others you meet the benefit of the doubt that you hope they would give you. Some great advice for making relationships work is to give people a chance to grow on you instead of looking for reasons to hate them.

God calls you to be different. Start looking for the best in people, and you'll usually find it. Instead of avoiding your enemies, find ways to spend time with them. Talk to them about some of your common interests. Ask for their help on something they do well. Find a way to work or play together. Don't gossip. If you can't talk about the problem face to face, no one else needs to hear you complain. Smile at them in the hallways, even if they don't smile back. Just think, even if it doesn't work, they may stay away because they think you are crazy.

> **"You have heard that it was said, 'You shall love your neighbor and hate your enemy.' But I say to you, Love your enemies and pray for those who persecute you. . . . for if you love those who love you, what reward do you have? Do not even the tax collectors do the same? And if you greet only your brothers and sisters, what more are you doing than others?"**
>
> MATTHEW 5:43-44,46-47 (NRSV)

We're not saying you have to pick your most difficult person to be your best friend, and we acknowledge that some people are evil and will not change. In spite of that, God does call us to try to be friendly. As Abraham Lincoln once said, "I don't like that man; I'm going to have to get to know him better."

Martin Luther King Jr. always strived to call men and women to radical love: "Christ did not seek to overcome evil with evil. He overcame evil with good. Although crucified by hate, he responded with aggressive love." If you treat no one as an enemy, they'll have a hard time keeping their own hates and fears alive. Don't expect quick changes.

It's easy to make enemies; it's noble work to make an enemy a friend. There is no more valuable reputation you can have than to be known as a good person. There may be times you run out of money, but you won't run out of deposits in your "people account." Never forget the wise words of Ben Franklin, "When you are good to others, you are best to yourself."

TALK IT OVER

1. Talk about one person in your life who is difficult to get along with. How might you turn that relationship around?

2. George Bernard Shaw said, "Do not do unto others as you would that they should do unto you. Their tastes may not be the same." Does treating other people well require that we know what they want and need? Or should we just give them what we would like?

3. Talk about different kinds of prejudice. What can you do to make a difference?

"Hating people is like burning down your own house to get rid of a rat."

HARRY EMERSON FOSDICK

Money: How Do I Get It and How Do I Keep It?

These may sound familiar: "We're not made of money!" "How much do you really need?" "When you have a job, you'll appreciate how much things cost!" "Do you think money grows on trees?" "Where's my change?" "Do I look like an ATM machine?" "At this rate, by the time you grow up, you'll owe us one million dollars."

Putting those frustrating conversations aside, one of the most important lessons we learn is how to manage money responsibly. You want to know the essentials such as: how to buy the things you want; how to save for the future; how to give to God and your church; and even how to spend some money just on having fun.

"Beware of little expenses. A small leak will sink a great ship."

BENJAMIN FRANKLIN

One truth remains: we can't learn to handle money unless we have some to handle. A Greek Proverb reads, "God gives the birds their food, but he does not throw it into their nests." Some of you may be lucky enough to have parents that drop an allowance in your nest. Be thankful. Other parents may require you to do chores to earn an allowance.

Some teens are expected to get jobs of their own. Even if you are given an allowance, you will learn quickly that most money is earned.

No matter how we earn our money, we all want to know how to spend it wisely. Ask your parents to let you know more about family expenses, how money is used to pay mortgages, phone bills, insurance, utility payments, food, clothing, medical expenses, and taxes. When you see what it takes to keep your family afloat, you will be better able to handle your own finances later. Remember though, family finances are a very private and personal matter. If you broadcast it around school, don't expect your lessons to continue.

> **"Students who worked less than twenty hours a week had a better chance of completing high school than those who worked more as well as those who didn't work at all."**
>
> OHIO STATE UNIVERSITY STUDY

Learning how to budget is important at any age. The next time your family takes you shopping for clothes, you might ask for a certain dollar amount you can spend. You may have to settle for the right of parental approval, but by having a budget to work with, you will be more aware of price tags and the value of a good deal. Learning to live by a budget while you are young will help you manage your money effectively as an adult.

Getting money from your parents is not the only way to learn about money. Working part-time will give you more money and more choices. Try not to let your work exceed twenty hours each week while you are in school. Work with your parents and your boss to set up a work schedule that will leave you the time and energy to do your school work and still have some fun.

Now that you have more money, what do you do with it? You may want to put some of your money into a savings account for your future. Like your parents, give some of what you earn to the church. Working hard earns you the right to spend some money on having fun and buying items that you can enjoy now. If you worked hard for the money you have, you probably won't want to waste it on things you don't need.

While we are talking about wasting money, keep your eye out for one of the biggest wastes of all: the big, bad "credit monster." Before you know it, this monster can suck you dry and keep you paying for a very long time. There is a way to control the "credit monster"; it starts with never accepting a credit card until you can afford one. Unless it is an emergency, use credit cards only to pay for those items or services you will be able to pay off by the end of the month. If you can't afford something, don't buy it until you have the money.

"If you think you want something, wait two weeks to get it. The purpose of this habit is to make you impulsive savers, not spenders."

HUMBERTO CRUZ

Centuries ago, Epicurus said an important truth: "Wealth consists not in having great possessions, but in having few wants." As the bumper sticker says, "He who dies with the most toys, still dies." Learn to be content with what you have instead of always having to buy the next bigger and better item. Frank

McKinley Hubbard's advice still works: "The safest way to double your money is to fold it over once and put it in your pocket." Even better, put it into your savings account.

An old American proverb reads: "Before borrowing money from a friend, decide which you need most." Keep these same thoughts in mind when friends want to borrow money from you. Some will pay it back, some won't. Make your conditions clear from the start, and set a time when any loan will be paid off. They won't always like your conditions, but good friends that plan on paying off what they borrow should not have a problem with your demands. If they do, let them borrow money somewhere else.

> **"An evil person borrows and never pays back; a good person is generous and never stops giving."**
>
> PSALM 37:21 (CEV)

All you have is a blessing and a gift from God. We can express our gratitude by giving to those in need, no matter how little or much money we have. You will find, as many have found before you, that what you give comes back to bless you.

TALK IT OVER

1. Have each person, teens and adults, answer: What are your main struggles regarding money?

2. Some experts suggest that teens who are in school full time should work at a job no more than 10 to 20 hours a week. Do you agree? Why or why not?

3. Some parents require their teens to give a portion of what they earn to the family. Some set that money aside for college expenses; others believe that working teens should also help pay for family expenses like food, shelter, and transportation. What do you think?

4. What percentage of your family income does your family give to your church or other charitable organizations? How do you feel about that amount? How would you like to see this money used?

5. What is a reasonable amount to set aside in savings every month by the parents? by the teens?

"Never lend people money—it gives them amnesia."

SOUPY SALES'S FATHER

Can I Have the Keys to the Car?

Believe it or not, in some ways your parents look forward to your driving. After all, who wants to be a chauffeur every day? For a while at least, you will love to do errands just to get a chance to drive. Long family trips won't seem so long when you can help with the driving. So when you drive responsibly, most parents will want you behind the wheel too.

Responsible is the key word. The image of one's child being a teen "road warrior," racing through the community with his or her car, gives parents nightmares—nightmares of traffic tickets, insurance-rate increases, and that dreaded call from the emergency room.

That's why, whether or not your state or school demands it, taking a driver's education and training course

> **"My dad didn't actually refuse to buy me a car. He just thought I ought to become more familiar with running simpler machines. He's letting me start on the lawn mower."**
>
> ANONYMOUS

is a good idea. The instructors will teach you the rules and provide driving experience, and when you complete the course, you may even reduce your family insurance costs. Trained instructors will probably do a better job than your parents could in teaching you to drive, and they are probably more relaxed. And if it doesn't go well, you won't have to face them over dinner.

On that glorious day when you do get your license, take the first step by talking with your parents about the ground rules before they ask you. Do you pay for gas and oil? for insurance? for your own traffic tickets? Know what is expected of you ahead of time.

Some things are worth doing whether or not your parents suggest them. Hitting the dashboard at 35 mph is like falling off a three-story building head first. Meaning . . .

> **"There's a way to help teens survive to become good drivers. It's simple. Have a bumper sticker that reads, 'If I'm driving irresponsibly, call my parents.' Then use a black marker to write the parents' phone number. Just knowing that you're driving around with your phone number visible to everybody will be an incentive to drive more responsibly."**
>
> FRED STENGLE

wear a seat belt. In fact, whether it is the law or not, make sure everyone in the car has his or her seat belt on before your foot hits the pedal.

A car can get you places, but it can also get people killed. The laws are not there to be broken; they are there to help keep your vehicle under control. When a car is not driven responsibly, it can be a lethal weapon.

You will notice quickly that not everyone obeys the laws of driving. Even if you drive safely, learn the value of defensive driving and staying alert. Act as if you're driving on the road with lunatics. Be

Safe Driving Tips

"Driving is merely a repetition of three basic actions: see, think, and do. Another way of saying this is: perceive, predict, perform. You must **perceive** trouble. You must **predict** what action is necessary. You must **perform** such action in time." The Smith System

"The Five Keys to Space Cushion Driving are: Aim High in Steering®; Get the Big Picture®; Keep Your Eyes Moving®; Leave Yourself an Out®; and Make Sure They See You®." The Smith System

"You are ready for defensive driving. There are things you can do to ensure a safe journey:

• Scan Ahead. Be ready to reduce speed and ascertain where you stand in the traffic flow.

• Check Behind. Be ready to take evasive action.

• Keep Your Distance. Leave enough space to avoid abrupt stops or lane changes in heavy traffic.

• Take Care At Intersections. Approach with your foot off the accelerator and over the brake pedal; look left, then right, then left again before proceeding.

• Practice Patience and Courtesy. The essence of defensive driving is the art of anticipating and avoiding hazards."

Stanley L. Englebardt,
"Drive Defensively—and Live"

prepared for the unexpected. Keep your eyes focused far down the road to anticipate traffic problems. Give ample distance between cars and think of moves you can make if problems occur. Safe driving means not letting your friends or your music become a major distraction. Keep your focus out your front window.

Now, let's talk about your car. You are only as good a driver as the car allows you to be. Learn how to check your tires, brakes, oil, and other vital systems. Preventive maintenance saves money in the long run. An honest mechanic will tell you, "Pay me a little now, or pay me a lot later."

So you have a car, a license, and some safe driving habits. One thing is sure to mess that all up—drinking and driving. As the famous blind musician Stevie Wonder has said, "Before I'll drive with a drunk, I'll drive myself." The life lesson here is simple: don't drive if you've been drinking, and don't ride with anyone who has been drinking. Too many teens and adults who felt they could handle their alcohol have been dead wrong.

> "In the annals of parent brutality (which include summer school attendance, forced feeding of fresh broccoli, and speaking to their kids in public), nothing is considered more inhumane to teenagers than taking away their cars."
>
> ERMA BOMBECK

> "Wine is a mocker and beer a brawler; whoever is led astray by them is not wise."
>
> PROVERBS 20:1 (NIV)

If you are at a party where you or your driver has been drinking, don't be afraid to call your parents for a ride home. They don't want anything bad to happen to you or your friends. If no one is home, call a taxi. A telephone call or a taxi fare, no matter how late or how much, is a small price to pay for your safety.

The legal age for drinking is twenty-one. But if you or your friends do drink, take the time to pick your designated driver, who wouldn't drink alcohol the entire time you are out. You may want to volunteer to take the role yourself.

What parents expect from you, they should do as well. Your parents shouldn't expect you to act responsibly if they don't act that way themselves. Ask them to promise to control their use of alcohol as well. You don't want to spend your evenings worrying about them either.

> **"Drive carefully—your car is not the only thing that can be recalled by its maker."**
>
> ANONYMOUS

Welcome to the joy and the responsibilities of driving. You'll like it, and sometimes it beats walking. By the way, if you clean your parents' car more often, they may even let you use it.

TALK IT OVER

Have both parents and teens answer these questions. Compare your answers and come to an agreement that both parties can live with.

1. What do you think is a fair way to handle car expenses? Who should pay for gasoline, insurance, and traffic tickets?

2. How will you handle the issue of drinking and driving?

3. What do you think are the most important elements of safe driving?

4. How should the use of the family car be determined.

Discuss the following contract and, if you agree to the provisions, have both parents and teens sign it.

Do you think it might help studying for the driving test?

You'd think failing the driving exam three times and watching his friends pass would supply all the motivation needed to actually force Sean to read the driver's guide before taking the test. But only after having to pay his own money for taking the test did Sean experience an attitude adjustment. On the fourth try a miracle happened; Sean passed.

Contract for Life: A Foundation for Trust and Caring

This contract is designed to facilitate communication between young people and their parents about potentially destructive decisions related to alcohol, drugs, and violence. The issues facing young people today are often too difficult to address alone. SADD believes that effective parent-child communication is critically important in helping young adults to make healthy decisions.

Young Adult: I recognize that there are many potentially destructive decisions I face every day and commit to you that I will do everything in my power to avoid making decisions that will jeopardize my health, safety, or your trust in me. I understand the dangers associated with the use of alcohol and drugs, and the destructive behaviors often associated with impairment.

By signing below, I pledge my best effort to remain alcohol and drug free and agree that I will never drive under the influence of either, or accept a ride from someone who is impaired.

Finally, I agree to call you if I am ever in a situation that threatens my safety and to communicate with you regularly about issues of importance to us both.

Young Adult Signature_____Date_____

Caring Adult: I am committed to you, and to your health and safety. By signing below, I pledge to do everything in my power to understand and communicate with you about the many difficult and potentially destructive decisions you face.

Further, I agree to provide for you safe, sober transportation home if you are ever in a situation that threatens your safety and to defer discussion about that situation until a time when we can both discuss the issues in a calm and caring manner.

I also pledge to you that I will not drive under the influence of alcohol or drugs and will always seek safe, sober transportation home.

Caring Adult Signature_____Date_____

Students Against Destructive Decision • Inc.

SADD and all SADD logos are registered with the United States Patent and Trademark Office and other jurisdictions. All rights reserved by SADD, Inc., a Massachusetts non-profit corporation. Copying of this material is prohibited unless written permission is received. SADD, Inc. sponsors Students Against Driving Drunk, Students Against Destructive Decisions, and other health and safety programs.

SADD, Inc., PO Box 800 Marlborough, MA 01752 Tel. 508-481-3568 • 508-945-3122

Who Needs Good Grades?

There is a place in the future for everyone, but it takes effort to find it. No matter what you end up doing with the education you get, you will get far more if you realize that all the work is for you. As a child of God, you have unique gifts, but your gifts need to be developed for you to reach your full potential. That's where your education comes in.

Now you might be thinking, "If God really wanted me to develop my gifts, he would have given me some good teachers." Not all teachers are created equal. You will have your share of good and bad teachers, but it remains your responsibility to find ways to work with each teacher you have. Be thankful for the good teachers, and find a way to work with the others.

> **"We are all born ignorant, but one must work hard to remain stupid."**
>
> BENJAMIN FRANKLIN

Learning how to learn is the most important skill, because your education won't end with high school or college. You will be learning all your life. God has given us an innate curiosity and a hunger for knowledge. Some people try to rest in what they have learned and forget to update their minds. You will probably have up to six different careers in your lifetime. Enjoy the learning you will go through in each one of them. Robert Solomon sums up the value of learning: "The mind is like a muscle, which no good American would admit neglecting—it must be exercised, stretched until it hurts a little, every day. In return it becomes stronger, more flexible, and more enjoyable to use."

Getting great grades in school is not a life and death issue, but it sure helps to have them. Straight A's will open many doors that would otherwise be closed to you. It could mean scholarships or getting into the best schools. In a competitive world, that can be an advantage worth working towards. But there are many other doors that do not require straight A's.

> "You can complain all you want outside, but inside this classroom you will apply yourself, and I will never teach down to you. One day, one of you little rascals may run for governor or president, and you will be prepared."
>
> MRS. SHELTON, JESSE JACKSON'S TEACHER

Don't be panicked or discouraged by a bad grade; it's not the end of the world. Learn to bounce back and apply yourself. There's no point like the present to do just that. If you have been struggling in school, there is no "right time" to turn your study habits around. The quicker you learn to develop the discipline of starting work early and doing some work every day, the sooner you will see it make a difference.

Procrastination is a problem for young and old alike. We recite the excuses in our heads that help us avoid anything we dislike doing. Maybe every time you even think about doing that English paper, your brain searches for the best available excuse— "I haven't got time to get into it!" "It's not due for two weeks; I'll have more time this weekend." "I'm too tired; my brain cells are zapped!" "I forgot the book in my locker." "I work best under pressure." Excuses help dull the pain and guilt of avoiding work, but only temporarily.

> "Try to please them at all times, and not just when you think they are watching. You are slaves of Christ, so with your whole heart you must do what God wants you to do. Gladly serve your masters, as though they were the Lord himself, and not simply people."
>
> EPHESIANS 6:6-7 (CEV)

You know the struggle, but what can you do? Not everything in life is fun or easy. We can expect some discomfort in doing things that are hard and things that aren't fun. How does knowing that help? Well, most of us have learned to avoid pain. Unfortunately, some painful and difficult activities in life still need to be done.

There is another secret that is equally important: Most things are worse in anticipation than they are in reality. Mowing the lawn, for example, is never quite as bad as the pain of anticipating having to do it. Getting any hated job done early usually is the best way to start your day. Hey, the bad is done; it's on with the good stuff. Avoiding work weighs you down. Getting it done frees you and gives you something to be proud of.

Here are a few tips on getting things done:

• Successful people break their work into small steps and then commit to completing each step on target dates along the way. You'd be unlikely to read a novel that didn't have chapter breaks to pace your reading. Once you have a plan, take the first step. Even fifteen minutes of work can get the ball moving. Once you're started, it's easier to keep it going.

• If you really want to get things done, let other people know what you are doing. When you tell others that you plan on working an hour on your term paper, they will remind you. That's not nagging, that's helping you do what you want done.

• Work, but don't work so hard you get sick of it. If you have put in a good hour of work, take a break. Reward yourself with an activity you like. After the break, you'll be refreshed and look forward to getting back to work.

> **"Ignorance doesn't kill you, but it makes you sweat a lot."**
>
> HAITIAN PROVERB

• Learn to live and work smart. If you're ahead of schedule on important work, you will feel better about taking time to enjoy life. No one likes to be so behind on their work that they have to pass up a good time. The payoff comes when instead of saying, "Sorry, I've got too much work to do," you get to say, "Sure, I'm caught up. Let's go!" If that sounds like a good deal to you, it's worth learning to work ahead on the things that matter.

Did anything come in the mail from school?

Getting to the mail first is a priority for any parent, particularly when your son has a history of changing an occasional D into a B, and progress reports are seldom statements of progress. They are more likely to be another invitation to grounding and time with mom and dad. Sometimes it seemed like Sean enjoyed grounding more than he liked making progress in English. Persistent limits paid off, but not without pain for parents and teen alike.

TALK IT OVER

1. On what tasks do you tend to procrastinate? What helps you get going?

2. Let the adults answer this one: In what ways do you have to get "good grades"? How are you evaluated?

3. What are the most important study habits you use that work for you?

4. What are you eager to learn more about? What does that say about your gifts that God may want you to develop?

"There will always be prayer in the schools . . . as long as there are final exams."

ANONYMOUS

Why Do I Have to Take Out the Trash?

B eing part of a family requires all to be responsible for doing their part to make living together work. The older you get, the more responsibilities you will have because you can do more, and it prepares you for a time you will be on your own. On the positive side, your help can, and does, make a difference.

Although *Webster's Ninth New Collegiate Dictionary* defines *chore* as "a routine task or job," those small jobs can add up to one very big chore if everyone doesn't help. One study suggested that the average person will spend four years of his life doing housework. That's quite an investment of time, and it ought not be the burden of any one parent or child. In short, not doing your chores makes home life an added chore for someone else. One family posted a sign on the kitchen pantry door: "If you drop it, pick it up. If you eat out of it, wash it. If you open it, close it. If you turn it on, turn it off. If you empty it, fill it up." Being responsible starts with not creating work for others.

> **"Sure, I run things at my house. My parents let me run the lawn mower, the washing machine, and the vacuum sweeper."**
>
> ANONYMOUS

Now, if you want to really impress your parents, do all your chores without their asking. When you take the initiative to meet your responsibilities without being asked, your parents won't have to "parent" you. They'll leave you alone more, see that you take initiative, and may even brag about you to other disbelieving parents. If you are forgetful, make a list of your chores and put it where you'll see it every day.

Whatever chores you do for your family, do a quality job. Doing a quality wash on the family car means doing the wheel rims and vacuuming, not just rinsing off the car. Tim McCarver once said, "Good habits are as easy to form as bad ones." It's your family home too; it deserves the best from everyone in the family.

> **"'A man had two sons; he went to the first and said, "Son, go and work in the vineyard today." He answered, "I will not"; but later he changed his mind and went. The father went to the second and said the same; and he answered, "I go, sir"; but he did not go. Which of the two did the will of his father?' They said, 'The first.'"**
>
> MATTHEW 21:28-31 (NRSV)

All chores do not need to be done alone. Some projects you can do together as a family. Whether alone or together, do all chores with a positive attitude, and they will go easier.

There's something else that comes with doing even the most disgusting chores— a sense of humility. In a world where people like to brag about their job titles, life in a home tends to bring us back to the basics. Knowing how to handle an overflowing toilet sometimes is far more important than the ability to make executive decisions.

God values all his children, and each person's labor done well to the glory of God is just as important in God's eyes.

But being responsible is more than doing chores. It means being part of the answer, instead of the source of the problem. For example, the use of the telephone can be a family problem. Besides the normal uses, it's there for emergencies for the whole family. Long calls can block access in emergencies. Take the time to talk as a family about phone guidelines. Come up with some that you are all comfortable with. By using the phone responsibly, you can avoid making it a battle zone.

> **"When my teenager learned that the telephone company's new fiber-optic cables can carry 40,000 conversations at once, he considered it a personal challenge."**
>
> ANONYMOUS

Take another look at the positive side of being responsible and in doing your part in the home. The more you know how to do, the better off you will be. When you move out, you will be ready and able to do everything in your own home. Then, someday, you may marry and have children who you can encourage to do their fair share.

> **"You cannot help men permanently by doing for them what they could and should do for themselves."**
>
> ABRAHAM LINCOLN

"I'm sorry I didn't get my chores done, but I had an accident. I was making my bed when I fell back in."

ANONYMOUS

TALK IT OVER

1. Let the adults answer this one: When you were a child, how were the household chores divided up?

2. Make a list of all the chores that need to be done to make your household run smoothly. How can the work be divided fairly?

3. What phone guidelines do you have in your home?

4. Let teens answer this one: What would you do differently in changing house rules and required chores when you have your own children?

What If I Don't Want to "Just Say No"?

Why do people use alcohol or drugs? Is it to celebrate, to have fun, to avoid problems, to get happy, to feel more relaxed with friends, to rebel against their parents, to experiment, or to impress others? Whatever the reason, there is no such thing as responsible use of an illegal substance, and it makes no sense to take or smoke anything that could harm your own body. Life can be confusing and no one is immune to problems and pressures, but no problem or pressure is worth becoming a slave to any drug.

You've probably heard about the abuse of alcohol and drugs until you're sick of hearing the warnings, so we won't make you go through them here. You know the facts, and you know friends who have abused drugs or alcohol and paid the price. You also know people who have experimented and not paid a price—yet. You might be saying, "There are also millions of adults who drink socially and never become alcoholics, so why can't teens enjoy alcohol like adults seem to do?" First, it's against the law. When you are of legal drinking age, the choice will be yours, as will the responsibility.

But the problem goes beyond the law; more of the problem lies in the addiction you can develop as a teen or an adult. How will you know? You wouldn't be considering it, if you weren't. The safest way to avoid becoming addicted is not to start. Making the decision to live drug free makes sense, but the commitment to stand firm has to come from within you. Only you can make that decision and show that you mean it.

Be strong enough to say no to drugs. Start by taking a stand in conversations when the subject of drugs and alcohol comes up. When people know what you think, they are less likely to ask you to join them. If they do, find a forceful message you are comfortable using that gets the point across. "No thanks. If you want to do it, that's up to you, but it's not for me." "No thanks. I like remembering my good times." "Hey, I may have to drive." If they persist, try being more direct, "I've already told you `no.' Back off on this." If all else fails, try blaming your family, "Look, I promised my folks" or "I promised my children." It may be hard to say no to your peers, but beating the habit once you're hooked on drugs or alcohol is even harder. True friends respect your right to be you. Likewise, as a true friend, you might want to help steer your friends away from substance abuse.

> **"Drugs are . . . an equal-opportunity destroyer. They have no conscience. . . . You're hear to make a difference, for yourself and those around you. So learn to count on each other. Take care of each other."**
>
> GEORGE BUSH

There is another benefit for taking a stand. By setting your own standards, you can become a positive model for others. By stating your limits you can provide strength to all those who want to say no, but don't have the courage to stand alone.

Ask God for the strength to stand firm. God calls our bodies the temple of God, so don't defile the temple by bringing in drugs. You are never alone. God is there to lean on during the tough temptations. Prayer can give you strength any time you call on its power.

> **"Drugs make you a liar and a cheat. Drugs take away your integrity, dignity, and character. I've worked . . . to get as much back as I can. And I'm going to continue to work the rest of my life to get it all back."**
>
> DEXTER MANLEY, NFL FOOTBALL PLAYER

There also is nothing wrong with seeking professional help if you need it. You can gain added strength, guidance, and support through caring people who are trained to help people with a drug or alcohol abuse problem.

Smoking is not only a waste of one's money, but it can harm your health later in life. A pack a day will cost you well over a $1,000 a year. Can you think of things you would rather spend your money on? The health cost you will pay for a smoking addiction is even more serious. If you are already smoking, take a look in the mirror the next time you light up. Ask yourself these questions: "Why am I doing this?" "Is it worth it?"

Don't expect stopping smoking to be easy. But it is achievable. Because smoking is still popular, you may have to say no to your friends. Try one of these responses: "No thanks, I have allergies." "No thanks, I'm in sports. And if the coach doesn't kill me for smoking, the workouts will." Finally, if you should choose to smoke anyway, do not smoke in your house or around people you care about. Passive smoke is not a gift anyone wants to receive, nor is it one you want to give.

"Don't destroy yourself by getting drunk, but let the spirit fill your life."

EPHESIANS 5:18 (CEV)

Don't forget your family when you have questions about drugs and alcohol. Try asking for their help, and you may be pleasantly surprised by how positively they respond. And one final thing, remember that you can have a good time without drugs, alcohol, and tobacco products. Take pride proving that you can make that choice.

RESOURCES

National Clearing House for Alcohol and Drug Information: 301-468-2600

National Institute of Drug Abuse Hotline: 1-800-662-4357

Parents Resource Institute for Drug Education (PRIDE): 1-800-853-7867

"A group of friends . . . decided . . . it would be more fun to get stoned. As they all started piling in the car, my head was contemplating. I said, `No thank you; I'm going to school.' As they drove off one way and I walked the other way, the feeling of accomplishment filled my body. With every step I took toward school, I felt strong that I was going to do something with my life, that I was going to be somebody. Just take one day at a time and I'll get toward where I want to go."

MARIBETH ALL

TALK IT OVER

1. What are the reasons you find most convincing for not using tobacco products, drugs, or alcohol?

2. As a Christian, how can your faith help you say no to tobacco products, drugs, or alcohol?

3. What statements do you have ready to say when approached by others who offer tobacco products, drugs, or alcohol to you?

4. How can you help your family and friends who have a problem with addiction? What can you say or do to make a difference?

5. What is a responsible use of alcohol for adults?

What If I Was Meant to Eat Desserts?

"Eat right." "Get out of that chair and get some exercise!" These are messages young and old alike get tired of hearing, but the truth remains: take care of your body, or it may not take care of you.

The sad truth is that, for most teens and adults, fitness levels are decreasing. Many people are not getting enough exercise. Too many people are eating junk foods promoted by athletes rather than becoming athletic themselves. That leaves making a positive change in your health habits to the most important person of all—YOU!

This isn't a call to run 50 miles a week. It isn't a crusade to banish all french fries and hot fudge sundaes. Being fit makes you more healthy. It doesn't mean having a body like a superstar athlete or a diet like a vegetarian monk. Aspire to that if you want to, but it is more important to develop some consistent exercise and eating habits that you can live with for the long haul.

"I know I need exercise, so would you mind running for me?"

ANONYMOUS

Ralph Waldo Emerson said, "The first wealth is health." Good health may not make you a lot of money or earn you a bunch of medals in sports, but it can give you a body that's ready to go. You can run a couple of miles, hike up a hill, or spend an evening dancing or playing basketball without having to have an ambulance ready.

You may have seen the bumper sticker that reads, "Life is uncertain; eat dessert first." It's important to enjoy every day, but you don't need to eat every dessert put in front of you.

> **"A vigorous five-mile walk will do more good for an unhappy, but otherwise healthy, person than all the medicine and psychology in the world."**
>
> DR. PAUL DUDLEY WHITE

If you haven't already done so, try developing a taste for healthy foods. Prepared correctly, a meal of fruits, vegetables, low-fat meat and dairy products, and whole-grain breads can actually taste great. Limiting the fat in your diet, does not mean eliminating every stop to your local fast-food joint; it just means you shouldn't stop every time you go by.

What about exercise? When asked if football is good exercise, former Oklahoma football coach Bud Wilkerson replied, "No. In football, there are twenty-two people on the field in desperate need of rest. And there are 50,000 people in the stands in desperate need of exercise." The same could be said about far too many teens and adults. It's a mistake to leave the exercise to the teams on the field. Research shows that people who exercise regularly have fewer colds, maintain their weight better, have a higher energy level, and live longer. Not a bad deal.

You don't have to overdose on exercise to get benefits. Instead, find something you enjoy and that you will do consistently. Doing too much too fast will put you on the road to burnout and injuries. Look for small ways to make a difference in your exercise habits. Associate with friends who like to exercise. Don't just watch sports; join a team. Instead of taking the car, ride your bike or walk. At least move more and move for longer periods of time and at a faster pace. If you like to eat, learn to like to exercise. People who regularly exercise burn more calories even when they are not exercising.

"You are the only person in charge of your body and your health. A program for fitness can't be just a fad. It can't be part of your way of life. It should be your way of life. Staying in shape and feeling your best isn't just for today—it can be forever."

CHER

Just remember, as the Olympic gold medal winner Bruce Jenner once said, "The only good exercise is one that you do." Making small changes in your eating and exercise habits now will make changes in your health today and even bigger changes later in life. Take care of your body, and it will take care of you. If your body is the temple of Holy Spirit, give God a nice home.

TALK IT OVER

1. Let each member of your family or group rate his or her health habits.

	Poor		Good		Excellent
Sleep and rest	1	2	3	4	5
Nutrition	1	2	3	4	5
Body Weight	1	2	3	4	5
Exercise	1	2	3	4	5

Share your results.

2. Identify the changes you would like to make in your health habits. How could your family help you make those changes?

3. What are your favorite healthy foods at home? What do you eat at fast-food restaurants?

4. When you think about developing an exercise habit you could do consistently, what comes to mind? What sports do you like to participate in and why?

"Do you not know that your body is a temple of the Holy Spirit, who is in you, whom you have received from God? You are not your own; you were bought at a price. Therefore honor God with your body."

I CORINTHIANS 6:19-20 (NIV)

If I Put All My Stuff Away, How Will I Find Anything?

"It wasn't my fault. Jim left my CD player outside." Even if true, excuses seldom resolve problems. When your car breaks down, it will do no good to tell a mechanic that it wasn't your fault. They may still demand payment before you get your car fixed. When you don't take care of your stuff, you may either have to do without it or even replace it. Both cost you money. As a result, it's worthwhile to learn the habit of taking care of your possessions.

There is an old saying, "Have a place for everything and have everything in its place." Developing a sense of order means being organized enough to help you and others find what they need when they need it. Few of us get overly excited about being organized, but all of us hate spending hours searching for important things we can't find. It's also no fun buying a replacement for something you lost. If saving money and time are not motivation enough, few will feel comfortable lending us their things if they do not see us take pride in taking care of our own possessions.

> **"My ultimate revenge— I hope you have eight kids and you live in a one bedroom house."**
>
> SHARON RIDING

Some teens may argue, "It's *my* room!" Parents keep saying, "But it's *my* house." There seems to be a self-fulfilling expectation that most teens are messy, but it doesn't have to be that way. And, of course, some teens are much neater than some parents. Perfect order and cleanliness make for dull people and wasted time, but total lack of order costs you daily.

If being a daily "neatnik" seems too much to ask, do your major cleaning once a week. After all, dirt needs a temporary home, too. Just understand that if you fail to take care of your room yourself, many parents will help you, but you may not like the price you have to pay to wage the battle.

> **"We have not passed that subtle line between childhood and adulthood until we move from the passive voice to the active voice—that is, until we have stopped saying 'It got lost,' and say, 'I lost it.'"**
>
> SYDNEY J. HARRIS

It is even more important to do your part to keep order in the rest of the house. After all, you share the house with some important people, namely, the rest of your family. Don't try one teen's guideline: "If it doesn't multiply, smell, catch fire, or block the refrigerator or TV, let it stay where it falls." That may be fine if you live alone, but not if you share space with others. One parent posted a sign in the family room: "Any item left unattended in the family room will be towed away and stored at the owner's expense." Don't let your family get to that point.

> **"Everyone who has something will be given more, and they will have more than enough."**
>
> MATTHEW 25:29 (CEV)

PAULSON FAMILY RULES

• *Clothes left unattended will be towed away at the owner's expense; after repeat infractions, they will be given to Goodwill.*

• *Parents are not on-demand chauffeurs; plan for a ride early or walk.*

• *Unless you are doing a science project, put your own rinsed dishes in the dishwasher before mold cultures grow.*

• *If the condition of your room does not reflect the views of management, shut the door until you have time to clean it.*

• *Do not borrow dad's tools unless you leave a valued possession to offer as collateral.*

• *An empty milk carton does not need to be refrigerated. Give it a new home in the trash.*

• *If you've lost your mind, think about the last time you used it and look there!*

1. Take a walk through your apartment or your house and yard. How does each person feel about the level of neatness or cleanliness?

2. Let the adults answer this one: What kind of rules did your parents have for how your room could look? How are your rules different for your children?

3. How much time do you spend each week cleaning? Is it worth it? What are the alternatives?

4. How can we be good stewards of the possessions God has given us?

What about the science experiment growing out of the bowl under your bed?

There seemed to be a force field that prevented Sean from getting plates of food out of his bedroom and back to the kitchen. In fact, alien life forms were known to grow in strange cultures that formed in bowls underneath his bed. Only the most determined ants seemed to be able to navigate the twisted journeys through the piles of clothes that were necessary to reach the cultures. Had it not been for the arrival of young women into his life, his habits may have never changed.

How Can I Become My Best Self?

I t's often been said, "Easy doesn't do it." Anything worthwhile in life is going to take work and effort. Yet, in movies, even the toughest problems are finished in about two hours. Then there are lottery winners who become instant millionaires. With that kind of programming, too many of us want everything yesterday.

One buys a surfboard visualizing himself riding eight foot waves with cameras rolling. After three hours of failing to find that elusive "sweet spot" and falling into the ocean, the board stays in the garage. That musical instrument that sounds so beautiful in the hands of a skilled musician, somehow doesn't work the same way when you buy your own and try to play it. The truth is it doesn't play itself. It requires fingers conditioned by hours of practice. Excellence in anything doesn't come quickly; it takes work over time.

The key to success echoes through three simple words: practice, practice, practice. Important victories

"Never try and teach a pig to sing. He can't sing, and it irritates the pig."

ANONYMOUS

in every area are won on the practice field first. Coach Vince Lombardi said it well, "Everyone has a will to win, but very few have the will to prepare to win." Even with practice, you will never win them all, but you can increase your batting average. Baseball teams pay a .300 hitter more than they pay a .200 hitter, but you don't get that kind of average by sitting in the bleachers. Victories in the real world come to the doers, not the observers.

> **"A lot of my passion for the game of football comes from my father Laird. My father said three things to us: Don't quit anything you start, work harder than the other person, and don't be intimidated by anything or anybody."**
>
> BILL COWHER, PITTSBURGH STEELERS COACH

You will never master everything, nor do you need to. Put your practice time into those things that are worth doing well. For most of us, being good at something always requires work and awkward moments of failure, but the masters keep bouncing back to try again.

> **"Everyone has a will to win, but very few have the will to prepare to win."**
>
> VINCE LOMBARDI

One private school in Hawaii requires every junior high student without medical limitations to run nine miles without stopping before graduating into high school. They increase their running mileage gradually so by the end of the year they all meet their goal and graduate. In high school, when students say, "I can't do it," teachers reply, "That's what you said about running nine miles." Such time invested in learning persistence through self-discipline is never wasted.

To find a job in the future, excellence will matter. Former Senator and NBA basketball star Bill Bradley advised, "Be prepared, or lose to someone who is." Learn on the practice field or in the classroom, but learn what you need to know.

When you have a God-given gift and you work hard to develop it, the victories will be yours and God's. Mastering any gift is never easy, but overcoming such obstacles makes achievement what it is—a real accomplishment. Welcome to the challenging pursuit of mastery—and the joy.

> **"Nothing in the world can take the place of persistence. Talent will not: nothing is more common than unsuccessful people with talent. Genius will not: unrewarded genius is almost a proverb. Education will not: the world is full of educated derelicts. Persistence and determination alone are omnipotent."**
>
> CALVIN COOLIDGE

"Do not neglect your gift, which was given you through a prophetic message when the body of elders laid their hands on you. Be diligent in these matters; give yourself wholly to them, so that everyone may see your progress."

I TIMOTHY 4: 14-15 (NIV)

TALK IT OVER

1. In what areas of life have you experienced the most success?

2. What would you like to be good at?

3. Where do you find the motivation to keep practicing on the tough days?

4. What is it about our culture that makes us so impatient?

What Can I Do for My Country?

As President John F. Kennedy stated, "Ask not what your country can do for you, but what you can do for your country." You can do something significant. When you get involved, you are more likely to feel empowered and enthusiastic. Look for like-minded people and make a difference together.

As citizens, you can celebrate the right and the privilege to live in a free country where you help choose the leaders that guide it. Everyone's vote counts. That is a privilege that was fought for and earned by men and women in ages past and is still being earned today. When given the chance, don't take their sacrifices lightly by failing to exercise your right and responsibility to vote. This means more than finding your local polling place. Responsible citizenship requires taking the time to study the candidates and the issues before voting.

> **"It may be that the greatest tragedy of this period of social transition is not the glaring noisiness of the so-called bad people, but the appalling silence of the so-called good people."**
>
> MARTIN LUTHER KING JR.

Some people ask, "Why study history?" Learning about history helps develop sound judgment and helps keep perspective in these challenging times. Former President George Bush knew that when he said, "The old ideas are new again because they're not old, they are timeless: duty, sacrifice, commitment, and a patriotism that finds its expression in taking part and pitching in."

For democracy to thrive, all citizens must exercise informed judgment. When you study history, you learn the tragic, the comic, the heroic, and the profound forces that have combined to make our country great. You come to understand how hard it is to preserve our heritage while still moving forward to make our country even better. If past generations have managed to do this, so can ours. Not only can we rise to the occasion, but we must.

> **"America is a symphony, not a melting pot. . . . In a melting pot, the ingredients soon lose their identity. In a symphony, each instrument is an integral part of the whole, adding its unique contribution to the movement, yet never losing its individuality, its tone, or its beauty."**
>
> WILLIAM ARTHUR WARD

Does one vote matter? Elections have been won and lost by small margins. You never know what race will require your vote. Don't limit yourself to TV ads in making your decisions; take time to be informed. Vote in all elections you know something about and not at all when you are not prepared or knowledgeable on the candidates or the issues.

We are given the right as citizens to say what we think. Write letters to your leaders when you have a strong opinion. Write letters when you're pleased with what they've done. Learn to be a supporter and a critic. No matter what your opinion of others and their positions, stand up for their right to say it, or you may someday have others try to take that right from you. William Allen White has written, "Liberty is the only thing you cannot have unless you are willing to give it to others."

Being a good citizen means doing your part for the environment. God has given us the right to use and the responsibility to take care of the world he has given us. God's dominion over nature always involved caretaking and preserving, not just harvesting. We were to be stewards first and users second. Are you ready to do your part as stewards of God's creation? Every year in the United States it is estimated that each person generates more than one ton of waste. Don't buy or use what you don't need, and be responsible in how you dispose of what you do use. Then keep doing it. You can't do everything, but you can make an impact by altering one habit at a time. Every day, do something to leave the world better for having been in it.

> **"For rulers hold no terror for those who do right, but for those who do wrong. Do you want to be free from fear of the one in authority? Then do what is right, and he will commend you."**
>
> ROMANS 13:3 (NIV)

Margaret Mead reminds us of the potential for involvement when she said, "Never doubt that a small group of thoughtful, committed citizens can change the world. Indeed, it's the only thing that ever has."

TALK IT OVER

1. What have you done so far for your country?

2. What are you proudest of as an American? What concerns you about our country? What can you do about those concerns?

3. What can your family do to be good stewards of the earth?

4. If you were to write a letter to the President, what would you say?

"If we wear out our earth, where are we going to live?"

DR. LAYNE LONGFELLOW

Write a Letter:
"If Only I Could Tell You..."

Hopefully, this book has helped you get beyond the lectures to actually talk about the things that really matter. But sometimes it can be easier to take a pen and a pad of paper to write down what you really feel. What would you say?

Here's one father and son's attempt to look back on the teen years.

Dear Sean,

When I first held you in my hands, there were tears of joy and concern. You were so small. There was relief when you finally were allowed to come home and be part of our lives. There was anticipation of all the dreams of what it could be like for all of us. There was even a little bit of fear. After all the books we read preparing us for having you, there was still this nagging doubt rolling around in the corners of our minds, "OK, the kid's here, what do we do now? For heaven's sake, he's depending upon us to do this right. Just don't mess him up!" I knew I didn't know how to be a parent; I was just hoping you would know how to be a good kid! No one could ever have prepared me for the joy, the pain, the frustration, the pride, the anger, and the love that has been a by-product of our journey together. Let me start by saying something I may not have ever taken the time to say: I'm so glad that we had you!

You know that I would never trade you for all the treasures in the world, but there were moments in our years together that I was tempted to trade you for far less. I'm sure the feeling was mutual at times. Even though you know that every family has its share of rocky moments, hurts, arguments, and disappointments, we just hope that by the time you begin your own family, you will have forgotten or forgiven most of the worst moments. Even better, I hope some of them will have become some of your best family stories. After all, perfect families exist only in parenting books. In a real home, there are no retakes, no ready warnings and no scripts to follow.

By now I hope you understand why we were tough on you at times. There was a simple reason for what we did; life as an adult isn't easy. To be ready for the challenges you would face, we cared enough to expect more of you. We all know there were parents who give their children everything they ask for; neither of us were that kind of parent. We never expected you to thank us at the time. But we do hope you have come to respect us. Even more important, we hope you have come to respect yourself.

That's enough of this seriousness; it doesn't match our family. We never seemed to let a day go by without sharing at least a few moments of laughter together. As we liked to say, "A family that laughs together stays together." We took time to laugh as a family, and we also took time to worship together. We hope by now that you have come to appreciate how God was so central to our family. Through the tough times, he will be there for you like he has been for us. He will be there through the good times as well. No matter what happens to your mother and me, let God continue to be your strength, your best counselor, and your best friend. Never let a morning pass without giving thanks for the gift of another day. Serve him, pray to him, and worship him. Do that, and you will never be alone.

You have learned many things from us. Take the best of what we have taught you, but don't let that limit you. Find your own unique path in life. When you find what you are meant to do, it won't feel like work. Don't settle for anything less. It is your own life to live; live it.

I'm glad you won't live your life alone. One of the greatest gifts life gives you is the opportunity to choose your own friends and your life partner. Because you choose them, that makes them very special to us as well. Nicole is special to us already. She fits in our family. The older I get, the more I love and value my own parents . . . and my grandparents, uncles, aunts, cousins, nieces, nephews, brothers and sisters. They are a network of love and support that makes family . . . FAMILY! Stay connected to your family. Take time to visit, write, call, and share your love. Be there for them; they will always be there for you.

When you were still young enough for me to pick you up and give you a big hug, I made you promise that you would never be too grown up to give your old man a hug. I knew you were too young to know what you were promising. Don't forget your promise. In fact, I hope neither of us ever forgets to say we love each other every chance we get.

There's one final message: I want you to know that I believe in you. Beyond all the past tough moments and frequent lectures, I am proud that you are my son. I am looking forward to seeing your future unfold in the years ahead. Stay close enough so that your mother and I get to watch it happen. I just hope that someday you will be able to say to me, "Dad, what you said to me growing up, you lived." Until that day comes, I will continue to try to walk my talk and to communicate in every way I know how that I will always love you.

Dad

Dear Dad,

I don't know if I have ever written down how I feel about you now that I'm out on my own. It is hard to find the right words, so I'll keep this pretty short. As a teen, I knew deep down that you and Mom really cared, but there were days when I wasn't always sure. It was the frustrating struggles over my school work that was the toughest to go through. I know now how right you were. I wish I had worked harder then, but I'm glad I'm back in school now. Sometimes it takes a while to get the message. I think I have it now.

I don't think I ever believed that life could be as hard as you said it was until I went into the army. I remember when I wrote home in my first letter, "All of the world is not Agoura Hills." That was a tough time, but I grew up a lot in that year. Your messages and letters meant more to me then as a young soldier. It helped me get through boot camp and my time in the service. My sergeant made your rules and discipline seem like kid's stuff, and I guess it was. But as a kid I still needed it. When I worked with young kids in the pre-school, I realized how many of them are not disciplined. It showed. You'd be proud of how many times I sounded just like you. Thanks for caring enough to discipline me.

I also want to thank you for taking me to church and for being involved in church. The friends and memories I made there are still important to me. Seeing how important faith is to both of you has helped God become more real to me. I still feel God may be calling me into the ministry, but there are many obstacles I will have to get over to make that a reality. God willing and with some effort on my part, it may yet happen. Whether it does or not, my faith is important to me. Like you, Nicole and I love to be a part of our church community. We try to make a difference working with youth where we can. Serving gives us much in return.

Dad, I have learned from you, and I respect you. I also hope with time you can learn from me as well. As an adult, I want you to respect me. That's why I have enjoyed working with you on this book.

I know family is important. We have too much fun together for it not to be. I know, we don't see each other as often as we used to, but I look forward to the times we do. I do love you dad. I love Mom too. Thanks for being there for me. I hope Nicole and I can do as good a job with our own kids as you both did with me. I guess there's not too much else to say, but a simple message—I love you.

Your Son, Sean

—•—

Time to Write

What would you put in your letter now? Let's find out. Take a pad of paper and a pen and find a quiet place to write. Compose a letter to your parents or to your children that communicates what you want to tell them. Take the time to share your letters and to talk about them.

"Hear, O Israel: The Lord is our God, the Lord alone. You shall love the Lord your God with all your heart, and with all your soul, and with all your might. Keep these words that I am commanding you today in your heart. Recite them to your children and talk about them when you are at home and when you are away, when you lie down and when you rise."

DEUTERONOMY 6:4-7 (NRSV)

About the Authors

Dr. Terry L. Paulson has been described as the "Will Rogers of management consulting." As a professional speaker and author, he helps leaders, teams, and the next generation of American workers to make change work. But few know his long background with youth, first as a teen youth worker with Young Life and many Southern California churches, and then as a licensed clinical psychologist. He knows the real world teens have to face as adults, on and off the job, and he also speaks their language today. He speaks to young and old alike on topics ranging from self-motivation to managing conflict and change. In addition to being a father and psychologist, he is author of the popular books, *They Shoot Managers Don't They?, Paulson on Change, Secrets of Life Every Teen Needs to Know, Making Humor Work, Meditations for the Road Warrior,* and *50 Tips for Speaking Like a Pro.* He is the 1998-1999 president of the National Speakers Association. You can get more information on Dr. Paulson through his office in Agoura Hills, California. You may contact him at: Paulson and Associates Inc., P.O. Box 365, Agoura Hills, CA 91376-0365, DrTerryP@changecentral.com, <http://www.changecentral.com>, 818-991-5110.

Sean D. Paulson has survived most of the Paulson family lectures without any noticeable damage. He graduated from Agoura High School in 1990. After a short stint in the U.S. Army, he attended college at Pacific Christian College in Fullerton, California. He continues his studies at Saddleback College in Saddleback, California. He has worked as an assistant director with the YMCA and as a pre-school teacher in Mission Viejo. As a teen, he was president of the Southern California Synod of the Youth Ministries Committee for the Evangelical Lutheran Church of America. He and his wife, Nicole, are both active in working with teens in the Youth Impact group at Lutheran Church of the Cross in Laguna Hills, California. With his father, Sean co-authored the book, *Secrets of Life Every Teen Needs to Know*. He is dedicated to helping teens and parents talk about the things that really matter.

Acknowledgments

The authors gratefully acknowledge the following sources for their contributions to this book. Any omissions are unintentional and will be corrected upon future printings.

Where Does God Fit into My Life?

Page 11: From an Ann Landers column, May 31, 1987.

Page 13: From "Here's to Dad, Who (Almost) Always Knows Best," *USA Today,* June 17, 1988, 4D.

Page 14: From *USA Today,* June 10, 1991, 3A.

What Does God Want Me to Do with My Life?

Page 16: From *Bits & Pieces,* Vol. N, No. 3, 1991, 16-17.

Page 17: From "Bird on Basketball," by John Bischoff, *Reader's Digest,* December 1987, 159.

Page 18: From "Denzel Washington Opens Up about Stardom, Family, and Sex Appeal," by Lynn Norment, *Ebony,* October 1995, 34.

How Can I Have More Self-Confidence?

Page 20: From *The Wit and Wisdom of Mark Twain* by Alex Ayers. © 1987 Harper & Row, 45.

Page 23: From *Peter's Quotations* by Dr. Laurence Peter. © 1979 Bantam Books, 448.

Why Should I Try Something Different?

Page 25: From "It's Always Too Soon to Quit," by Lewis Timberlake, *Plus*, April 1989, Vol. 40, No. 3, Part II, 17.

Page 26: From "An Anthology of Student Motivational Quotations," by Isadore Rosenberg, Ph.D., Pierce College, 1989, 41.

Page 27: From *Top Performance*, March 1987, Vol. 2, Issue 1, 10.

How Can I Make It through the Bad Days?

Page 28: From a Dear Abby Column, December 28, 1986.

Page 29: From "Never Be Late for Lou Holtz," *Meeting News*, February 1989, 79.

Page 30: From *Plus*, May 1988, Vol. 29, No. 4, Part I, 9.

Page 31: From *The Humble Warrior* by Evander Holyfield and Bernard Holyfield. © 1996 Thomas Nelson Publishing, 26.

What's So Funny?

Page 35: From *Soundings*, May 1989, 3-4.

Page 36: From *The Wit and Wisdom of Mark Twain* by Alex Ayers. © 1987 Harper & Row, 36.

Page 37: From "Finding Humor in Yourself," by Sherri Dalphonse, *Correspondent*, July/August 1995, 15.

How Can I Talk So My Parents Will Listen?

Page 40: From *Great Quotes and Illustrations* by George Sweeting. © 1985 Word Books, 94.

How Can I Find Real Friends?

Page 44: From *Great Quotes from Great Leaders* by Peggy Anderson. © 1990 Celebrating Excellence Publishing, 63.

Page 45: From "An Anthology of Student Motivational Quotations," by Isadore Rosenberg, Ph.D., Pierce College, 1989, 15.

Page 46: From *Great Quotes and Illustrations* by George Sweeting. © 1985 Word Books, 243.

Page 47: From "My Greatest Lesson," Anna Muoio, editor, *Fast Company*, June/July 1998, 83-92.

Who Needs Good Manners?

Page 50 (top): From "Such Is Life," by Jeanne Perkins Harman, *Readers Digest*, 1998.

Page 50: From "Table Manners for the Power Hungry," *USA Today*, March 22, 1988, 5D.

Page 51: From "The Shy Child," *Family Circle*, September 1, 1981, 104.

Page 52: From "Here Are Some Table-Top Etiquette Tips to Avoid Dinner-Party Disasters," by Barbara Nachman, *Reno Gazette-Journal*, July 22, 1989, 4D.

You Want Me Home by When?

Page 55: From *The International Thesaurus of Quotations* by Rhoda Thomas Tripp. © 1970 Harper & Row, 546.

Page 56: From *Readers Digest*, March 1987, 24.

Did You Say "Sex"?

Page 59 (top): From "Who Says You Can't Teach Abstinence?" by Mona Charen, *Conservative Chronicles*, April 23, 1997, 9.

Page 59 (bottom): From "Quotelines," *USA Today*, September 10, 1990, 12A.

Page 62: From *The Oregonian*, January 27, 1987.

Page 63: From "Who Says You Can't Teach Abstinence?" by Mona Charen, *Conservative Chronicles*, April 23, 1997, 9.

If Everybody Else Lies, Why Should I Tell the Truth?

Page 64: From *The Wit and Wisdom of Mark Twain* by Alex Ayers. © 1987 Harper & Row, 36.

Page 65: From *Great Quotes from Great Leaders* by Peggy Anderson. © 1990 Celebrating Excellence Publishing, 21.

Page 67: From *Great Quotes from Great Leaders* by Peggy Anderson. © 1990 Celebrating Excellence Publishing, 63.

How Can I Get Along with People?

Page 69: From *The Passionate State of Mind and other aphorisms* by Eric Hoffer. © 1955 Harper & Row.

Page 71: From *Peter's Quotations* by Dr. Laurence Peter. © 1979 Bantam Books, 236.

Money: How Do I Get It and How Do I Keep It?

Page 72: From *Great Quotes from Great Leaders* by Peggy Anderson. © 1990 Celebrating Excellence Publishing, 45.

Page 73: From "Teaching Teens the Work Ethic," by Gloria Byron, *American Way*, March 1, 1988, 14-18.

Page 74: From "Credit Card Pitfalls," *USAA Magazine*, August/September 1996, 28.

Page 76: From "Here's to Dad, Who (Almost) Always Knows Best," *USA Today*, June 17, 1988, 4D.

Can I Have the Keys to the Car?

Page 78: From "Check Teens' Driving Habits," by Sheila Taylor, *News Chronicle*, January 2, 1989.

Page 79 (top): From "The Five Keys to Space Cushion Driving." Trademarks and written excerpts are property of the Smith System Driver Improvement Institute, Inc. Used by permission.

Page 79 (bottom): From "Drive Defensively–and Live," by Stanley L. Englebardt, *Readers Digest*, November 1987, 81-84.

Page 80: From "Teens with Licenses Drive Parents to Act," by Erma Bombeck, *Los Angeles Times*, June 15, 1989, V4.

Page 81: From *Soundings*, June 1989, 3.

Page 83: From "Contract for Life." © SADD, Inc. Used by permission.

Who Needs Good Grades?

Page 84: From *Ben Franklin's New Almanac* by Neil Wyrick, quoted in *Sharing Ideas*, August/September 1987, 27.

Page 85: From "Nourish the Appetite to Learn and Grow," by Jesse Jackson, *Los Angeles Times*, September 10, 1989, V5.

Page 87: From *Readers Digest*, October 1987, 11.

Why Do I Have to Take Out the Trash?

Page 91: From *Great Quotes from Great Leaders* by Peggy Anderson. © 1990 Celebrating Excellence Publishing, 23.

What If I Don't Want to "Just Say NO"?

Page 94: From "Don't Look Other Way, Bush Urges," *USA Today*, September 13, 1989, 6A.

Page 95: From "Sports View," by Bob Woolf, *USA Today*, December 4, 1990, 10C.

Page 97: From "High School Confidential," by Linda Gross, *Los Angeles Times Magazine* May 31, 1987, 19-37.

What If I Was Meant to Eat Desserts?

Page 99: From "An Anthology of Student Motivational Quotations," by Isadore Rosenberg, Ph.D., Pierce College, 1989, 12.

Page 100: From "Body by Cher," by Cher and Robert Haas, *People*, January 21, 1991, 85-90.

If I Put All My Stuff Away, How Will I Find Anything?

Page 103: From *The International Thesaurus of Quotations* by Rhoda Thomas Tripp. © 1970 Harper & Row, 392.

How Can I Become My Best Self?

Page 107 (top): From *Sport*, November 1998, 47.

Page 107 (bottom): From *Dictionary of Sports Quotations* by Barry Liddle. © 1987 Routleage & Kegan Paul, 171.

Page 108: From *Sharing Ideas*, October/November 1989, Vol. 12, Issue 1, 32.

What Can I Do for My Country?

Page 110: From *SoftPower! Newsletter (#5)* by Maria Arapakis, January/February 1989, 10.

Page 111: From *Plus*, October 1988, Vol. 39, No. 8, Part I, 11.